It is not uncommon for corporations to pay $80,000 to air a one-minute advertisement on television. Even in a society known for its inflation this is a lot of money for just sixty seconds. Executives know, however, just what one minute of communication can do to sell their products. They consider such expenditures reasonable if not inexpensive.

In religious circles we have always placed greater value on the quantity of time spent praying than on the quality. But Jesus said, ". . . when ye pray, use not vain repetitions, as the heathen do: for they think that they shall be heard for their much speaking" (Matt. 6:7). This does not make it any less necessary to get alone with God for long stretches of time, but neither should we ever forget the value of our minutes with God. This book was written to make each minute with God count. Each devotion can be read in sixty seconds, and this should be helpful to busy people. I pray that this book will bless you and that all of us will increase our appreciation of every moment we spend communing with and meditating on our Lord.

1 Bucket of Water

Ask, and it shall be given you; seek, and ye shall find; knock, and it shall be opened unto you. (Matt. 7:7)

In the middle of a lake near Akron, Ohio, is an island that was once the site of a famous amusement park. Shortly after the park lodge was first constructed one hundred years ago, it caught fire. Fire fighters rowed to the island to fight the blaze. A candy vender working on shore wanted to do his part, so he filled a bucket with water, rowed to the island, tossed it on the burning structure, and rowed back to shore for more water. It never occurred to him to use the lake water.

While we laugh at the candy vender, many men try to solve their problems in much the same way. Divine help is available, but they ignore it and struggle to solve the human dilemma with human wisdom. After all their exhausting efforts the fire still burns and little is accomplished.

If we question this premise, we need only look at the recidivism rates in our prison systems. Sixty to ninety percent of those coming out will return within five years. Yet we still try to rehabilitate without a spiritual perspective. How much wiser we would be to dip deeply into the resources Christ offers to change men. This is true not only with the problems of our society, but also with our personal needs.

2 Show the Way

Then the devil leaveth him, and, behold, angels came and ministered unto him. (Matt. 4:11)

Appalled by the rising illiteracy rate in the United States, the government decided to launch a campaign to get people to read. One of the brainstorms of the official campaign was to place a sign in all the buses of San Francisco: "Illiterate? Write today for free help." Needless to say, the campaign did not improve matters much, because those who needed to read the sign could not.

God understood from the beginning that posting signs for spiritually illiterate people will not suffice. Therefore, He planned to send His own Son into the world to show men how to live. Christ then died and rose again so men could be free from the power of sin and death. No other way would work. Earthlings simply could not read and understand the signs of the Law or the Prophets. They had to be shown. So Christ came.

Looking at the earthly life of our Lord, we learn so much about how to live. We can learn one of the most powerful lessons from the way in which He handled temptation. Satan attacked Him when He was weak and hungry. Yet Christ rebuffed the attacks of Satan by skillful use of God's eternal Word. Against such testimony Satan does not have a chance. Let us today look closely at every situation in the life of our Lord and learn how we too are to act and react.

3 Heart to Heart

Now the end of the commandment is charity out of a pure heart, and of a good conscience, and of faith unfeigned. (I Tim. 1:5)

Ralph Waldo Emerson lovingly visited the grave of his young wife every day for two years after her death. And though his was one of the greatest intellects of the day, ordinary people learned to love him for his sentiment and honesty. One New Englander said, "We are a simple folk here, but we understand Mr. Emerson because he speaks our language." And he did speak their language. His lofty ideas and deep intellect never were wasted in arrogance or conceit.

In his letter to young Timothy, Paul insisted that Timothy always speak to the hearts of the people. He said some false teachers who had come into the church delighted in using high-sounding words and impressing everyone with their knowledge. Timothy was never to do this. Rather his life and lips must overflow with love, a good conscience, and a genuine faith.

Each of us has a specific work to do for our Lord. Perhaps yours is to teach or occasionally preach. Most likely it is just to share Christ with friends one-to-one. It is vital that we remember Paul's exhortation to speak to people's hearts. We do this by being honest and open with them. We need not impress them with our great knowledge; we need only touch them with our love.

4 Improving the Preacher

I exhort therefore, that, first of all, supplications, prayers, intercessions, and giving of thanks, be made for all men. (I Tim. 2:1)

The Scottish pastor John Carmichael, serving his first church, was young and very frightened. He felt that he was doing badly and that his people were looking at him with pity and contempt. One day, to his terror, the stern elders of the flock filed into his vestry. "Next Sabbath," they told him, "before you begin to speak, we ask you to say to yourself, 'They're all loving me.' And it's true, we will all be loving you very much." That meeting changed the young preacher's life, and today he is recognized as one of the finest preachers Scotland ever produced.

Paul understood the pressures of the pastorate. He also understood that people could be a tremendous blessing to young Timothy as he tried to lead the church at Ephesus. Therefore, Paul told Timothy to admonish the people first of all to pray for their leaders. Praying people produce good pastors.

This advice is still good. And it goes for all men in positions of leadership. Before we criticize them, judge their actions, or disagree with their decisions, we are first to pray for them, intercede on their behalf, and thank God for them. We must always temper our complaints with prayers. May we pledge today to pray, as God's Word demands, for all those in authority.

5 Hope

. . . according to his abundant mercy [God] hath begotten us again unto a lively hope. . . . (I Peter 1:3)

Several years ago serious lung cancer threatened the life of entertainer Arthur Godfrey. Godfrey says, "Over the years I've developed a pretty good sense of optimism—even about the weather. 'What a lousy day,' people sometimes gripe. Not me. When you've lived as long as I have, and survived as much, every day you draw breath is borrowed time and, therefore, a great day." Godfrey's attitude is a healthy one because, as writer John Buchanan says, "Without optimism there can be no vitality."

Earthly optimism may relieve some tensions. There comes a time, however, when even this cannot carry man beyond the barrier he faces. This is where spiritual optimism comes in. The Bible calls it hope. Hope is one of the three graces of the Holy Spirit: "And now abideth faith, hope, charity, these three. . . ." (I Cor. 13:13).

While the greatest of the graces is love, hope still has a vital role in the life of the believer. And God's Word tells us to hope for three things: God's calling (Eph. 1:18), eternal life (Col. 1:5), and the resurrection (Acts 23:6). Believers are to be optimistic. Our lives do not end at the grave. And we are assured that "all things work together for good to them that love God, to them who are the called according to his purpose" (Rom. 8:28).

6 Invisible Cages

For he shall have judgment without mercy, that hath shewed no mercy; and mercy rejoiceth against judgment. (James 2:13)

Birds live in invisible cages. While we often say someone is "free as a bird," all birdwatchers know that the conduct of birds is rigidly fixed. They are prisoners of the land they fly over and slaves to the air they fly through. John and Jean George told of a wild cardinal they saw die because he could not break through this invisible barrier. He was strangled on a piece of property that was cleared of trees and plowed under. They said, "Almost all birds live and love and die behind bars of nature's compulsions. They are captives in cages of their own instincts, from which, with rare exceptions, they cannot escape."

Birds are not the only creatures locked behind invisible prison bars. James tells us that some people are lost through bitterness. He plainly says we can obtain mercy from God only as we are merciful: "For he shall have judgment without mercy, that hath shewed no mercy. . . ." On the other hand those who have learned to forgive are free because "mercy rejoiceth against judgment."

Those locked in the invisible prison of an unforgiving spirit will never be free. Those who have sought forgiveness from Christ, however, have found they first must forgive. In letting go their anger they find real freedom. Forgive someone today.

7 Liberated

Being confident of this very thing, that he which hath begun a good work in you will perform it until the day of Jesus Christ. (Phil. 1:6)

Michelangelo saw the task of the sculptor as that of freeing figures from their marble prisons. In each block of stone he saw some "person," and he chipped away until that form emerged. Sometimes he failed, as with St. Matthew. This famous statue is only half finished because Michelangelo could not get the stone to release the figure of the brilliant apostle.

Paul saw God as the Sculptor who is freeing men from the prisons of their carnal natures. He wrote to the Philippians that God was doing a great work in and on their lives, and encouraged them to have confidence in His work. He assured the new believers that God is perfectly capable of "finishing" us as He desires for His and our greatest good. This master Sculptor never gives up, and no prison is too strong for His skilled eye and learned hand.

In yielding ourselves to the direction of the Master, we are "being filled with the fruits of righteousness, which are by Jesus Christ, unto the glory and praise of God" (Phil. 1:11). All believers should remember that today's bumps and bruises may merely be the Master chiseling, working away at our lives until we are conformed to the image of His Son. Thus we relax even though the chisel may bite, for we know His work is sure and the result to be well worth the moment's inconvenience.

8 London on Fire

For I know that this shall turn to my salvation through your prayer, and the supply of the Spirit of Jesus Christ. (Phil. 1:19)

Fire raged for five days through the wooden structures of London, burning 13,000 buildings, including 89 churches, and doing thirty million dollars worth of damage. The death toll was staggering in that disaster about 315 years ago. Although the memory of London's holocaust has faded, it brought sweeping changes which still affect us today, changes like building codes, fire-insurance companies, and fire protection and prevention.

Pain most often brings change. Paul recognized this. In Philippians 1 he talked about people who were preaching with impure motives and bringing him personal pain. Yet he was confident that from this bad situation two things would occur: first, the name of Christ would be heard by many who had not heard it before; next, the Philippians would earnestly pray and that would bring many blessings to them, the church, and Paul.

Just as did the London fire, Paul's sufferings made people aware of the need for preventional protection; they were awakened to their tasks. On this day we would be wise to remember our priorities. Let us also pray that the gospel will be preached around the world.

9 Legend of Fear

. . . and in nothing [be] terrified by your adversaries. . . . (Phil. 1:28)

An ancient legend of India tells of the "spirit of plague" passing an old man sitting under a tree. The man asked the spirit, "Where are you going?" The spirit answered, "To Benares to kill one hundred people." Later the man heard that ten thousand had died in that city. When the "spirit of plague" came by again, the man said to him, "You lied! You said you would only kill one hundred people." "I killed but one hundred," replied the spirit, "fear killed the rest."

Paul says much about fear. He told Timothy, "For God hath not given us the spirit of fear; but of power, and of love, and of a sound mind" (II Tim. 1:7). And he reminded the Philippians not to be terrified of their adversaries (1:28). Although the enemies of Christ might make believers uncomfortable physically, they cannot destroy the eternal soul. Believers need not panic in the face of pain or threat.

Ever practical, Paul specified things the Philippian believers were to do: first, their behavior was to be becoming to the gospel; then, they were to stand together in the faith as one body and to strive for the gospel. This is excellent advice for us in our strife-filled world. May we bring glory to the gospel, stand together in love, and constantly seek to be better Christians.

10 Death Sentence

Look not every man on his own things, but every man also on the things of others. (Phil. 2:4)

Loo Ching migrated to the United States from China several years ago, and soon after his arrival he violated a fundamental law of the Tong Soon. The council met and sentenced him to death, but American laws forbade the sentence to be carried out. So the leaders simply decreed Loo Ching a dead man. From then on no one spoke to him. Shopkeepers would not sell him food. Children turned the other way when he came down the street. His room was rented to another and his belongings put in the alley. He could not speak English and knew nothing of American ways. Each day he grew thinner until one morning he was found dead in the snow outside a tea shop.

People need people. In the tragic case of Loo Ching, his death sentence was effectively carried out when people withdrew their love. Paul says relationships are important. He encourages believers to consider others in everything they do. One can never withdraw his love from others and remain a believer.

"Am I my brother's keeper?" Paul tells us we are to be concerned for others. He also reminds us to hold others in higher esteem than we do ourselves. In other words, we are to invest our love and concern in those about us. We must remember that our Christian responsibility is both vertical and horizontal: to God and to others.

11 Forget the Face

Let this mind be in you, which was also in Christ Jesus. (Phil. 2:5)

Charles William Eliot, one of the great presidents of Harvard University, was born with a serious facial disfigurement. Once he was old enough to be sensitive about it, his mother said, "My son, it is not possible for you to get rid of this handicap. We have consulted the best physicians and they can do nothing for you. But it is possible, with God's help, to grow a soul and mind so big that people will forget to look at your face." This is exactly what he did, and today he is recognized as one of the educators who shaped modern secondary education.

Paul talked about the only begotten Son of God willfully coming to earth and humbling Himself to become a man. He further subjected Himself to the disfigurement of the cross. Yet Christ lived so purely and died so obediently that today we no longer remember the shame of the cross. Rather, His life, death, and resurrection force us to look beyond that ugliness to the glory of His salvation. One day every knee will bow before this Lord of lords.

Christ is our example of obedience. The challenge is clear. Our lives are to bring glory to His name. Paul said, "Let this mind be in you, which was also in Christ Jesus." We, like Eliot, can live lives so beautiful and meaningful that people will look beyond our human form to see the living Christ within us. May that be our prayer for this day.

12 Direct Order

Do all things without murmurings and disputings.
(Phil. 2:14)

A cantankerous old lady came through surgery with flying colors. The surgeon sternly told her when she awoke, "In accordance with the rules of this hospital, you will have to walk ten minutes the very first day, and you will be out of here in a week since hospital beds are at a premium." On her first day the old woman took her steps as ordered and within a few days was walking all over the hospital. Later her family tried to pay the doctor a bonus for his work.

"Nonsense," he said. "It was just a routine operation."

"It's not the operation we're marveling over," said the grandson. "It's her walking. She hasn't taken a step in six years!"

Some people apparently respond to direct and firm orders. In his Philippian letter Paul gave several direct orders that leave no room for argument. One of the sharpest was "Do all things without murmurings and disputings." This advice is not always easy to take, but it is Holy Scripture.

Paul said "all things." This means not only religious things, but even menial tasks of the day such as washing dishes, mowing the lawn, and carrying out the trash. Paul said we must obey this order so "that ye may be blameless and harmless, the sons of God, without rebuke, in the midst of a crooked and perverse nation, among whom ye shine as lights in the world. . . ." (Phil. 2:15).

13 Used and Abused

For all seek their own, not the things which are Jesus Christ's. (Phil. 2:21)

Cherub-faced Bobby Driscoll won the hearts of Americans in the Walt Disney movie *Song of the South.* His life ended in tragedy, however, when his body was found on March 30, 1968, in an abandoned tenement. Beside him were empty beer bottles. He had died from years of drug abuse. Shortly before his death at age thirty-one, Bobby said, "I was carried on a silver platter and then dumped into a garbage can." He was bitter because those who liked him as a child actor cared nothing for him when he could no longer entertain them.

Too often men traffic in human flesh, seeking what people have or are rather than genuinely loving them. Paul noted that two men who traveled with him sincerely loved the people of Philippi. Of Timothy Paul said, "For I have no man likeminded, who will naturally care for your state." Of Epaphroditus Paul wrote, "For he longed after you all. . . ." These men really cared for people.

Most people in our world are reaching out for sincere friends. They need people who love them as they are rather than for what they have or for their prominent positions. Believers must see people as people, being neither awed nor appalled at their veneer. Today let us form lasting and loving friendships as did Timothy and Epaphroditus.

14 To Make a Mirror

For we are the circumcision, which worship God in the spirit, and rejoice in Christ Jesus, and have no confidence in the flesh. (Phil. 3:3)

Madame Chiang Kai-shek tells of a young Buddhist monk two thousand years ago who looked pious, clasped his hands, and chanted "Amita Buddha" all day, believing he could thus acquire grace. One day the Father Prior of the temple sat beside him and began rubbing a piece of stone against a brick. This went on for several days until the young monk asked, "Father Prior, what are you doing?"

"I'm trying to make a mirror," he replied.

"But," protested the youth, "you cannot make a mirror of a brick."

"That is true," the old man replied, "and it is just as impossible for you to attain grace by chanting all day."

This ancient Chinese story points to the truth that sinners cannot become saints unless their character changes. Paul understood this and frankly told the Philippians to have no confidence in the flesh, that is, not to consider themselves worthy of salvation because they had gone to the right schools, memorized the right things, and chanted the right prayers. Paul learned this from personal experience, because he had done all these things and they had not saved him.

Salvation is a divine interruption in man's heart. In Christ we are made new creatures and become totally dependent not on our own fleshly righteousness but on His grace. As the songwriter said, "Jesus paid it all, all to Him I owe."

15 Prophetic Poem

. . . if by any means I might attain unto the
resurrection of the dead. (Phil. 3:11)

After Dag Hammarskjöld's untimely death in an
airplane crash, friends found a prophetic poem in his
family Bible. Hammarskjöld had translated it when but a
schoolboy. The poem simply said:

The day you were born, everybody was happy—
you cried alone.
Make your life such, that in your last hour
all others are weeping,
And you are the only one without a tear to shed!
Then you shall calmly face death,
whenever it comes.

Hammarskjöld so lived, and the world wept at his
passing.

Preoccupied with Christ's resurrection, Paul seemed
to stretch so he might be worthy of the great price paid
for his salvation. He admitted that he had not yet
attained a state of perfection, but said he was seeking
daily to be led of the Spirit and to grow in the Lord. He
added that he forgot past mistakes and failures, and
pressed on "toward the mark for the prize of the high
calling of God in Christ Jesus."

Paul's honesty and healthy ambition inspire us in our
pilgrimage. The wise person is the one who strives
toward perfection in Christ. Although we may not be
perfect, we are daily growing up into Christ. To do this,
we, like Paul, must "be found in him, not having mine
own righteousness, which is of the law, but that which is
through the faith of Christ. . . ."

16 Just Honk

. . . and if in any thing ye be otherwise minded,
God shall reveal even this unto you. (Phil. 3:15)

A Catholic priest told of driving behind a car with the
message "Honk if you love Jesus" on a bumper sticker.
"I don't exactly approve of that sort of thing," he said,
"but maybe it was the nice weather or something."
While stopped behind the car at a traffic light, the priest
honked and waved. The lady in the car stuck out her
head and yelled, "Can't you see the light is red, stupid?"
The priest laughed and said, "It serves me right."

This incident reminds us that we often are tempted to
act out of character with our Christian witness. In the
heat of busy days we sometimes say or do things that are
not a good testimony for the kingdom. The lady's
attitude was wrong, and she probably later regretted it.

Paul squarely approached the problem of being
human. He admonishes us always to act like believers
and reminds us that when we do not, God can and will
call this to our attention. If the lady driver was a sincere
believer in Christ, she was convicted of her sin and asked
forgiveness from Christ. It is wonderful to realize that
God loves us so much He demands our best. He makes us
uncomfortable when we do wrong and tells us how to
correct it. God's Word, Paul said, is "profitable for
doctrine, for reproof, for correction, for instruction in
righteousness. . . ." (II Tim. 3:16).

17 Innocent Victims

For our conversation is in heaven; from whence also we look for the Saviour, the Lord Jesus Christ. (Phil. 3:20)

The horror of Hitler often overshadows that of Mussolini. We must never forget, however, how evil this little dictator was. He marched without mercy on Ethiopia and machine-gunned peaceful people who still hunted with bows and arrows. He stayed in power for twenty-one years by murder, intrigue, and exile. When German forces collapsed in 1945, the escaping Mussolini was caught and, along with his mistress, shot. Their bodies were taken to Milan and hung by the heels in front of a garage. It was an ugly end to an ugly and totally immoral man.

There are evil men in the world and some even in the church. Paul warns the Philippians of some false teachers "whose end is destruction, whose God is their belly, and whose glory is in their shame, who mind earthly things." Their end, like Mussolini's, will be disgrace and damnation.

Pitted against the evil ones of this world are those who, like Paul, can say that their "conversation is in heaven." These are men who live for eternity rather than the few years between birth and the grave. They refuse to live by the law of the jungle—"Survival of the fittest"—but seek to fulfill their responsibilities to God and man. May our conversation be rooted in eternity rather than in the gutters of this earth.

18 Public Rebuke

*I beseech Euodias, and beseech Syntyche, that
they be of the same mind in the Lord.* (Phil. 4:2)

The same day the disastrous Chicago fire broke out, a
forest fire started in Peshtigo, Wisconsin, which killed
five hundred more people than the Chicago blaze. Called
the worst natural disaster in history, the Wisconsin fire
started when many small fires were sparked in the dry
weather. The Chicago conflagration received more publicity because it caused far more property damage and
because of the romantic story of Mrs. O'Leary's cow
beginning the Chicago blaze. The fact is, both fires were
devastating.

Much attention had been given to the false prophets
within the early church. However, Paul saw another
potential danger to the young church—a disagreement
between two ladies in the assembly. Apparently the feud
had reached such proportions that it threatened to
consume the little church. Paul insisted that drastic
measures be taken.

Never one to back away from problems, Paul insisted
that other believers help the ladies settle their dif-
ferences. Often we need others to help us see our
problem from a different viewpoint before we can
solve it. We must remember that left unattended, our
little fires of anger can bring destruction and even
spiritual death.

19 The "Thank-you Cure"

. . . but in every thing by prayer and supplication with thanksgiving let your requests be made known unto God. (Phil. 4:6)

A wise old doctor in South Wales often prescribes the "thank-you cure." When a patient comes to him depressed but without symptoms of serious woes, the doctor tells him, "For six weeks I want you to say 'Thank you' whenever someone does you a favor. And to show you mean it, emphasize the words with a smile." When the patient complains that few do him favors, the doctor simply replies, "Seek and ye shall find." Six weeks later the patient usually returns with a new outlook, freed of his grievances against life, convinced that people have suddenly become more kind and friendly.

There is grace in gratitude. God's Word is filled with admonitions to thank Him for the things in our lives. This is where praise begins. The wise believer has learned to begin and end all prayers and supplications with thanksgiving. In doing so we are more aware of the goodness of God and the kindness of others.

Praise does far more for us than it does for God. Our Father is not some egocentric being who needs to be told constantly how wonderful He is. He desires the praise of His people because it opens their hearts to God and their fellow man. The grateful heart is a gracious heart. We are to season our requests with thanksgiving, and in so doing our love for the Lord grows deeper.

20 Mind Advertisement

. . . for I have learned, in whatsoever state I am,
therewith to be content. (Phil. 4:11)

Famed author Bruce Barton has wisely said: "For
good or ill, your conversation is your advertisement.
Every time you open your mouth you let men look into
your mind." Jesus said the same thing many years
earlier: ". . . for out of the abundance of the heart the
mouth speaketh" (Matt. 12:34). It is true that to know
how people think and what they are, we only need listen
to their words.

Take Paul, for example. The famous apostle said,
". . . for I have learned, in whatsoever state I am,
therewith to be content." Paul knew how to be abased
and how to abound. In other words, the circumstances
of his life did not affect his happiness. Rather, his joy
was firmly rooted in a relationship with the Lord he
loved. In such confidence Paul could frankly claim, "I
can do all things through Christ which strengtheneth
me."

It would be well to listen to ourselves talk today. Is
our conversation laced with positive faith or negative
doubt? Does it expose a mind that is thoroughly
saturated in love for Christ or in the things of this
world? Our strongest witness for Christ is a positive
conversation that breathes hope.

21 The Sea Cares

. . . no church communicated with me as concerning giving and receiving, but ye only. (Phil. 4:15)

At sunset a little girl sat with her father at the edge of the ocean watching the tide come in. The waves sent a sheet of molten gold across the dry sand, almost like a caress from the arms of the sea. In that magic moment the daughter said dreamily, "Isn't it wonderful how much the sea cares about the land." Telling about the incident, the father said, "She was right. The land was merely passive. But the sea cared—and so it came."

Caring costs. It means reaching out to help when others pass by. Paul knew the cost and comfort of such care. Philippi had been the only church that had seen his physical needs and relieved them. They would forever occupy a special place in his heart. He did not have to ask for their help. They saw and they reached out. Thus he promised them, ". . . my God shall supply all your need according to his riches in glory by Christ Jesus."

Most of us say to someone in need, "If I can help, please tell me." The loving person does not even ask. He moves to relieve the person's needs and touch him with his concern. Caring does cost, but its rewards are eternal. May we look around today and really see the needs of others. Then may we relieve those needs in a practical and loving way. This brings blessing to both giver and receiver.

22 The Pebble

... the trying of your faith worketh patience.
(James 1:3)

"A small trouble is like a pebble," Celia Luce has said. "Hold it too close to your eye and it fills the whole world and puts everything out of focus. Hold it at the proper viewing distance, and it can be examined and properly classified. Throw it at your feet, and it can be seen in its true setting, just one more tiny bump on the pathway to eternity." Wise words from a wise woman.

James encourages us to keep trouble and even temptations in their proper perspective. In the sadness or passion of the moment, we often have them pressed to our face where we can see nothing else. They are constantly in our thoughts and overwhelm us. We need to cast them at our feet and remember God can and will use them to make us better believers. The trying of our faith does, as James said, produce patience.

Most of us are like the kindergartner who planted a tiny seed in a small flower pot and dug it up every day to see how it was doing. We must learn to "let patience have her perfect work, that ye may be perfect and entire, wanting nothing." One believer joked, "I want patience and I want it right now." Too often we think like that. May we relax and put the pebbles of tribulation and temptation in their proper place. We need not be dominated by them, and through Christ we can conquer them.

23 In the Teeth of Death

If any of you lack wisdom, let him ask of God,
that giveth to all men liberally.... (James 1:5)

"In one hand I have a Bible, and in the other a
pistol," the communist guard said, taunting Salvation
Army Commissioner Herbert Lord. "I despise your God.
Let me see you prove His power. Pray to Him to tell you
which hand holds the Bible and which the gun. If you
are wrong I will kill you." Lord lowered his head. "Have
you prayed?" the guard asked. "Which hand did your
God tell you?" "I did not ask," the Christian said. "For
two things only I prayed: that God help me keep my
temper and for strength to die decently." The guard's
face twisted in anger and he took aim with his gun.
Then, frustrated, he turned away.

The firm resolve of Commissioner Lord is shared by
many believers in deep crisis. God has provided a
resource to His children which no other humans have.
When we face trials, James tells us to ask for divine
wisdom and promises that God can and will give it. As
the communist guard was frustrated, so the enemy of
our souls will be by the wisdom Christ gives.

Although we are not facing a firing squad, the
promise is still ours. If we but ask for spiritual direction,
God will supply it. In every decision today may we seek
His perfect will for us.

24 Died a Grocer

Let the brother of low degree rejoice in that he is exalted: but the rich, in that he is made low. . . .
(James 1:9, 10)

Asked to explain the meaning of an epitaph he had written for his tombstone—"Born, a Human Being; Died, a Wholesale Grocer"—the businessman replied, "I was so busy selling groceries I did not have time to get married and have a family. I was successful. But I was so busy making a living, I never had time to live." Many today have a similar problem.

James points out that life is just a vapor and we must spend our time doing important things. He reminds us that the man born in low circumstances can be exalted through Christ and that those born in riches should rejoice because they can enter the door of eternal salvation. The door is open to all men without preference. The only key is faith in Christ.

We often need to be reminded that we are creatures of eternity, not of time. We must consider our actions not in terms of our few short years on this globe, but of that day when we will stand before our Creator and account for the deeds of the flesh. May we constantly remember that we were born human beings and that we need not die in despair. Through Christ we can and will live forever. Let us not be so busy making a living that we forget to make a life.

25 Aversion Therapy

But every man is tempted, when he is drawn away of his own lust, and enticed. (James 1:14)

Aversion therapy is a rapidly growing and intensely controversial way to change human behavior. This therapy rests on the premise that you can punish undesirable behavior over and over until the patient so links the behavior and the punishment that he gives up that behavior. Those who want to quit smoking are given electrical shocks every time they pick up a cigarette. The drinker who desires to stop is either shocked or so chemically treated that a drink makes him physically ill. This therapy does not attempt to get at the root of behavior; it merely conditions a person's actions.

While the new form of therapy sounds good, it will never really work since change must come from within, not from external pressures. James pointedly said the problems of behavior spill over from the heart. Temptations are temptations only because the person has first been drawn away by his own lusts. Obviously the best therapy is to have a change of both heart and head through Christ.

Understanding this, the believer looks to Christ for inner strength against evil. Then there is something each of us can do: "Wherefore lay apart all filthiness and superfluity of naughtiness, and receive with meekness the engrafted word, which is able to save your souls" (James 1:21).

26 Men of Action

But be ye doers of the word, and not hearers only, deceiving your own selves. (James 1:22)

"I want my religion like my tea—hot!" proclaimed General William Booth, founder of the Salvation Army. In 1865 he set up his first tiny mission for down-and-outers in London. Booth's officers used shock methods to win converts. They charged into gin palaces and dragged drunkards out. They gained public attention with all the tricks of a circus barker. One poster told of "men who were once wild as lions, savage as tigers . . . who were prowling through the black jungles of sin, but captured by our troops and tamed."

While one may disagree with Booth's methods, there is no doubt his efforts affected modern history. The Salvation Army is today a monument to a man so dedicated to his Christ that he did something about rescuing the perishing. James said that men of faith are men of action, not just of words.

In a colorful word picture, James noted that if we look into God's Word and do nothing about what we see there, we are like a man who looks into a mirror and then forgets what he saw. Practical Christianity involves doing something about cleaning up our own lives and reaching the lost.

Maybe we need a few more William Booths in our century, men who like their religion "hot" with active service to their Master. Real believers are not merely hearers; they are doers.

27 A Bum's Advice

But if ye have respect to persons, ye commit sin, and are convinced of the law as transgressors. (James 2:9)

Several years ago Alfred Hitchcock, the famous motion picture director, was on location in a New York slum when inclement weather brought the filming to a halt. A filthy old man sidled up to Hitchcock and said, "I have a suggestion. Why don't you rig up some artificial light." Hitchcock patiently explained to the derelict why this was impossible, treating him with great respect. Asked about it later, Hitchcock said, "Ideas come from everywhere, including left field. You have to listen or you're lost."

This act went beyond kindness and took account of human potential, however low the light is burning. James tells us that believers must treat all men alike. We are often so impressed with the rich that we forget they have hungry hearts like the rest of us. We are tempted to like them for what they have or who they are. Or we are so disgusted with the shabby that we turn them off. The wise believer realizes that both are God's children.

If we show preference for the rich, James warns, we transgress the law. Believers are to love all men alike. May we pray today to see men as men, not as types or in social brackets. This is real Christian love.

28 Critical Dimensions

For as the body without the spirit is dead, so faith without works is dead also. (James 2:26)

In building the huge Arch of St. Louis, dimensions were so critical that surveyors had to work at night when the temperatures on all three walls were the same. Each measurement had to be exact. In pouring the foundation of either leg, a mistake of only 1/64 of an inch would have been disastrous. That difference in the angle of the top of each foundation would be multiplied until the two fingers reaching toward the sky would have failed to meet. All of the careful work was worth it, and the Arch today is a fitting monument to the opening of the West and to the ingenuity of man.

Like the two towers of the Arch, faith and works reach toward each other. In church history there have been miscalculations as to the importance of each. Some emphasized works so much that the Reformation had to call Christendom back to faith. On the other hand, mere faith is not enough, James said. Both legs of the tower must meet for the structure to be complete.

Theologians will continue to disagree on the proper balance of faith and works. While the battle rages, we laymen merely need to ask God's Holy Spirit to help us maintain a proper balance of faith and works. Faith and works can be combined in proper proportion to where our lives will be monuments of blessings.

29 Little Things

Out of the same mouth proceedeth blessing and cursing. My brethren, these things ought not so to be. (James 3:10)

Little things can mean a lot. The jerking of a panful of frogs' legs when touched by a knife led to the discovery of dynamic electricity. The trembling lid of a teakettle was the beginning of the steam engine. A spider's web across the corner of a garden inspired the suspension bridge. A lantern swinging from the dome of a cathedral suggested the principle of the pendulum, by which time is measured. An apple falling from a tree revealed the law of gravity. And a cow kicking over a lantern caused the devastating Chicago fire.

James considered little things so important that he spent almost a whole chapter talking about the destructive fires of evil the tongue can ignite. He said frankly, "If any man offend not in word, the same is a perfect man, and able also to bridle the whole body." He warned that believers cannot continue to spew forth words of blessing and of cursing. The conversation of the Christian is changed at conversion.

We are eternally at war with our tongue. It is like a wild and untamed horse that we must ride constantly to keep it from disrupting and destroying relationships. Today it would be well to give special attention to this powerful instrument. While we each ask God for a thousand tongues to praise our great Redeemer, let us each control the one we have.

30 Two Steps Behind

From whence come wars and fightings among you? come they not hence, even of your lusts that war in your members? (James 4:1)

"The chief tragedy of the human race," Sydney J. Harris says, "is that the war approaching always seems necessary and inevitable. It is only 20 years later that it is seen as avoidable and futile. Is the mind perpetually condemned to live two steps behind the passions?" Tragically it seems so, even in our modern society. Lewis Mumford, historian and philosopher, says, "The dark age is not coming—we are in the midst of the dark age."

Nowhere else in literature is there such a clear statement of the cause of all wars as in the Book of James. James pinpointed the source of all conflicts, whether they be personal, ecclesiastical, or national: the lusts in our hearts. War will be with us until our hearts change.

While historians might think James's statement too simplistic, perhaps we should consider all battles in the light of the apostle's statement. On the personal level we find that conflicts arise from selfishness or insistence on our own way. According to James, friendship with such a worldly spirit is enmity with God. If we are friends with this type of spirit, we are enemies of God. May our desires be tempered today with His will, and then our lives will not spill over into feuds and fights, but will bring healing to men.

31 What Can I Do?

Draw nigh to God, and he will draw nigh to you. . . . (James 4:8)

During the recent energy crisis we seemed so helpless. Then the New York Daily News showed how each of us could save energy: "One less hour a day of color TV saves a fourth barrel of oil a year. One less washing machine load saves a half barrel. One less clothes dryer load saves a third barrel. Using the dishwasher once for every two present uses saves three and a half barrels, while using the air conditioner one less hour from May through September saves a half barrel." There is something we can do.

James tells the believer some things he can do to make his life more like Christ's. While Jesus is the Author and Finisher of our faith, there are practical steps we can take to be more aware of His working and more suitable to His service. James suggests, for example, that we submit ourselves to God and resist the devil, that we draw near to God so that He will draw near to us.

James adds that we should not speak evil of one another or say arrogantly that we will do as we please. We are in God's hands, not ours. We are to do good because "to him that knoweth to do good, and doeth it not, . . . it is sin." With such a list we have a lot to work on today in our lives. There is something we can do, and may we do it.

32 Violence

Ye have condemned and killed the just; and he doth not resist you. (James 5:6)

Every sixty-eight seconds between 1820 and 1945 a man died at the hands of a fellow man as a result of violence. Six hundred years before Christ, Ezekiel said, ". . . the land is full of bloody crimes, and the city is full of violence." The scene has not changed much since then. While 200,000 scientists and engineers are working in military-related jobs, only a handful are working to stop the violence in our land.

The problem of violence has been with us since Cain killed Abel. By all logic we should be able to control the passions that spill over into violence. Even in our modern society, however, we seem helpless in the face of the killer instinct. The Bible says violence is a result of sin, and as long as man refuses to repent, we will reap the whirlwind.

Although the situation is discouraging, there will come a day when all the scores are settled. James told of the time when those who have used power to harm their fellows will be judged sternly. These acts of violence never go unnoticed, and while man may escape punishment here, there will be a judgment day. In our violent society may we pray for the coming of Christ, who will once and for all abolish violence with His rule of love and peace.

33 Handel's *Messiah*

Be ye also patient; stablish your hearts: for the coming of the Lord draweth nigh. (James 5:8)

Handel wrote his *Messiah* in just over three weeks. Working morning, noon, and night, he hardly touched the food set before him. After finishing part 2, which contains the "Hallelujah Chorus," he rushed to the window and cried, "I did think I did see all heaven before me and the great God Himself." Those who have listened to that inspired piece of music would add a resounding "Amen!" to the great master's sentiments.

In the midst of a crooked and perverse generation, James reminds us, our Lord will break through the clouds and call us to Himself. All of the sufferings, privations, and sorrows of this world will fade when we view the glory of the Messiah. No doubt our hearts will burst out in a new song. James encourages us to keep in mind those things that await the faithful and to be patient until that day.

Thousands of years of history have proved that we need divine direction and rule if we are ever to become what God created us to be. So much of our history has been marred with wars and heartbreak. That will all change when Christ comes. He teaches us to pray, "Thy kingdom come." May that prayer follow us through this day and may we also be patient until our Lord comes.

34 The Rocking Chair

. . . the effectual fervent prayer of a righteous man availeth much. (James 5:16)

A woman who reared a large family and ran a boarding house at the same time was asked how she remained so composed. "Well," she said, "you know that big rocking chair in my room? Every afternoon, no matter how busy I am, I go up there to rock awhile and empty out my brains." While this is good therapy, there comes a time when we need to do more than empty out our brains; we need to empty our souls. This is why James closed his important letter with a strong admonition to pray.

Prayer is far more than pouring out our woes. We do not speak to the air when we make our petitions. There is One who listens and is touched by our infirmities. Therefore, to keep a healthy spiritual life we must consider prayer our privilege and responsibility.

James 5:16 tells us to pray if we are afflicted, to seek prayer from our brothers and sisters in the Lord for our illnesses and problems. James also reminds us that Elijah was a man of prayer who suffered the same frustration we do. What marked him as a great man of God was his practice of prayer. Indeed, "the effectual fervent prayer of a righteous man availeth much." Today may we be ones who pray. Only then will we accomplish great things for the kingdom.

35 Surprising Statistics

*And take heed to yourselves, lest at any time
your hearts be overcharged with surfeiting, and
drunkenness, and cares of this life....* (Luke
21:34)

While we Americans complain about the soaring food
prices, we pay a smaller percentage of our income for
food than people of other nations. Statistics released by
the *New York Times* indicate that Americans spend
approximately 17.6 percent of their income for food, as
opposed to 21.9 for Germans, 26.5 for the French, and
22.3 for the Japanese. Other peoples of the world are
even more desperate. In India 60 percent of a person's
income goes for food, while in some parts of Africa, 70
percent.

Life in an affluent society raises unique problems.
Americans must decide how to use their money wisely.
This is no problem in countries like India and Africa
where necessity dictates. But we must remember that, as
Jesus said, much is required of the one who has been
given much.

Christ's words of warning in Luke 21:34 are most
appropriate for the West. In the last days we are tempted
to waste our substance rather than use it wisely. Jesus
told us to shun excess, drunkenness, and the cares of this
world. In our materialistic society we are to maintain a
proper perspective and to look for His coming.

36 Best Investment

For the word of God is quick, and powerful, and sharper than any twoedged sword. . . . (Heb. 4:12)

When John Wanamaker was eleven years old, he bought a Bible. In later years he said, "I have made many large purchases in my time involving millions of dollars. But the purchase of that Bible was my greatest buy. I paid for it in small installments. Looking back over my life I see that little book was the foundation on which my life has been built, and the thing that has made possible all that has counted in my life. I know now it was my greatest investment and the most far reaching and important purchase I ever made."

Wise men recognize the value of God's Word. In prayer we speak to God, and through His Word He speaks to us. The writer of Hebrews said God's Word is quick and powerful, sharper than any double-edged sword, "piercing even to the dividing asunder of soul and spirit, and of the joints and marrow, and [it] is a discerner of the thoughts and intents of the heart."

James called the Word a mirror. In it we see ourselves and also what we can be in Christ. By reading the pages of Holy Writ, we grow up into Christ in all things. The sincere believer will make God's Word part of his daily diet. Even though parts of the Bible may be hard to read, it is best if we read all parts. May we vow today to carry His Word with us and use it every day.

37 Denial

. . . Lord, I believe; help thou mine unbelief. (Mark 9:24)

Bennett Cerf tells about the London plutocrat who, driving his new Rolls Royce through the Alps, heard a disquieting snap. The front spring had broken. He called the Rolls plant, and they flew a new spring to him as well as mechanics to install it. Six months passed and the Londoner received no bill. He went to the plant and asked about it. After a brief delay the manager appeared, gazed at him reproachfully, and announced, "There must be some mistake, sir. There is no such thing as a broken spring on a Rolls Royce."

Many people treat doubt as the plant manager did the broken spring. They deny its existence and try to talk themselves into some pseudofaith. This seldom works, however. A better way of handling doubt is that of the father who brought his child to Jesus to be healed. When Christ asked, "Do you believe?" the man admitted, "I believe; help thou mine unbelief." His child was healed.

Jesus honored the man's request because he lived in the arena of his faith rather than the house of his doubt. He had come to Jesus even though he did have doubts. God understood and healed. Honesty is always the best policy. If we open our hearts frankly to the Lord, He always hears and heals.

38 Love at Home

Nevertheless let every one of you in particular so love his wife even as himself; and the wife see that she reverence her husband. (Eph. 5:33)

Legend tells of an attractive young couple who boarded a train for the traditional honeymoon at Niagara Falls. They were very much in love, and that was apparent to all who saw them. Suddenly the bride found herself hurling insults at her husband, and his rejoinders matched hers in bitterness and venom. Then she discovered a stranger sitting next to her whose presence had caused the transformation. "How did you get in here?" she gasped. "And who are you?" The stranger softly answered, "I'm Ten-years-from-now."

Many marriages are under stresses that threaten to destroy them. The sweetness of the honeymoon has worn off, and the business of living has caused some abrasions. Paul understood these problems, and he spent much time admonishing husbands and wives. Here is his formula for a happy home and a lasting marriage.

There must be one leader in the home, and God ordained the man to be that. But the man has a spiritual obligation to deeply love his wife as his own body. Both are to cling to each other rather than side against each other with relatives. The admonition to love is so strong that Paul repeated it again and likened the husband-wife relationship to that of Christ and His Church. In today's prayer period, let us pray for a deeper love in our homes.

39 From Us

*Cast thy bread upon the waters: for thou shalt
find it after many days.* (Eccles. 11:1)

Two shipwrecked men were marooned on an un-
inhabited island in the South Pacific. They had been
there for many months, living off roots and berries,
when they saw a bottle floating in on the tide. They
shrieked with joy. With trembling hands they uncorked
it to get the note inside. When they saw the note, their
faces fell. "Nuts," one of them exclaimed. "It's from
us."

This illustrates that whatever we throw out will
eventually come back to us. This is the premise of
Ecclesiastes 11:1. The farmer's fields were flooded, but
he sowed anyway. When the waters receded, the seed
grew and the crop came.

There is an eternal law of sowing and reaping. If we
are merciful, we obtain mercy. If we sow to the flesh,
we, like the flesh, are destined for corruption. If we sow
to the spirit, we receive eternal life. Therefore, we
continue to sow good seeds for the kingdom although it
now seems fruitless to do so. Solomon was wise in
saying, "In the morning sow thy seed, and in the evening
withhold not thine hand: for thou knowest not whether
shall prosper, either this or that, or whether they both
shall be alike good." Our job is to sow faith; it is God's
job to make the crop grow.

40 No Longer Blind

. . . one thing I know, that, whereas I was blind, now I see. (John 9:25)

A Virginia woman is now able to see for the first time since 1900. Josephine Mulkey had been blind since an accident at age six. A recent operation, however, restored vision to her and she said, "It makes me so happy that I feel like singing 'How Great Thou Art.' " One of the most pleasant surprises, said Mrs. Mulkey, was seeing what a beautiful family she had raised. Her grandchildren and neighbors had looked much like she expected "but much prettier." She added, "Everything I look at is so pretty."

The ecstasy Mrs. Mulkey experienced is the same felt by the man who, having been blind from birth, was healed by Christ. The man was so enraptured by the new world around him that he was totally uninterested in the accusations of Jesus' enemies. He answered their accusations with this: "Whether he be a sinner or no, I know not: one thing I know, that, whereas I was blind, now I see."

We who have been released from spiritual blindness get impatient with the critics of Christ. Our personal experience tells us that He indeed is the Messiah, and the arguments of the agnostics and the athiests seem silly to us. We once sat in darkness, but now we have seen a great light. When we experience something, we are never at the mercy of those who argue against it.

41 Sing a Song

Let every thing that hath breath praise the Lord.
Praise ye the Lord. (Ps. 150:6)

Tradition tells us that Ambrose, the fighting bishop of Milan, introduced singing into the European church. In A.D. 380 the church was rent with heresy, and the devout kept "watch day and night in the church, ready to die with their bishop . . . singing hymns and psalms so they would not succumb to weariness and grief." Today we have more than 400,000 hymns in the English language, and new ones are being written every day. God's Word tells us we are to praise God in song.

Much of Christianity's vitality lies in its hymns. When we get together for worship and sing unto the Lord, His Spirit draws us to Himself. Charles Wesley, a great hymnist, knew the power of sacred song. In his pocket hymnal he tells us how we should sing: "Sing all. Join with the congregation as frequently as you can. Let not weariness nor weakness hinder you. Sing lustily with a good courage. Above all, sing spiritually. Have an eye to God in every word you sing. Aim at pleasing Him more than yourself. So shall your singing be such as the Lord will approve of."

This is good advice for us. God desires that we worship Him in song. "Let every thing that hath breath praise the Lord. Praise ye the Lord." Today is a day to sing praises to our Savior.

42 Hunger

. . . and there shall be famines, and pestilences, and earthquakes, in divers places. (Matt. 24:7)

Observers predict that within a few years the most crucial issue will be hunger. Because world demand for food is rising rapidly, our ninety-day stockpile in this country has dwindled to one for twenty-seven days. Scientists predict that one major crop failure would result in the worst famine this world has ever known. Adding to the problem is the unequal distribution of food: the average person in poor countries consumes about four hundred pounds of grain a year; the average North American eats about a ton, at least one hundred pounds of which is in the form of whiskey and beer.

James Reston says, "The rich world doesn't really believe in the coming food crisis any more than it believes in the oil crisis. One day we will all be weight watchers." A famine is already spreading in Africa, and the hunger in India has long been known. Famine should not surprise believers since Jesus foresaw it, predicting an increase of famine before His return.

Our world is desperate. In these troubled times the believer must not panic and seek shelter from the hurts of humanity. He must go forth to share the Christ who can solve these problems and guide man through the trying days ahead. Christ is coming soon!

43 Caring Counts

The Lord give mercy unto the house of Onesiphorus; for he oft refreshed me, and was not ashamed of my chain. (II Tim. 1:16)

A famous jeweler once sold a magnificent ruby to a customer after one of his salesmen had failed. Asked how he did it, the jeweler said, "My clerk is an excellent man and also an expert on precious stones. There is just one difference between us. He knows jewels, but I love them. I care what happens to them and who wears them. The customers sense this. It makes them want to buy—and they do." Not only with jewels but with all aspects of life, caring counts.

Paul, writing his last will and testament to young Timothy, praised Onesiphorus and asked that Timothy greet him. This young man had sought out Paul while he was in prison. Onesiphorus was not ashamed of Paul's chains and spent time encouraging him. He did this not just out of Christian duty, but out of a real love for the Lord and for Paul. His caring counted.

Today we will probably be asked to perform some act of Christian love for our church, our neighbors, or our families. May we learn to do these things not just because they are expected of us but because we really care, and may we convey that to those to whom we minister. People can sense when we really are concerned for their spiritual welfare and not just interested in them as a statistic or out of duty. May we strive today to be an Onesiphorus.

44 Selfless

Ye are my friends, if ye do whatsoever I command you. (John 15:14)

The plane carrying Dr. Frederick Banting, a famous physician-scientist, crashed in a snowstorm in a forest near Musgrave Harbor, Newfoundland. One of Banting's lungs was punctured by crushed ribs, but he used his waning strength to bandage the wounds of the pilot, the only survivor. Then he lay down on the pine boughs in the snow and went into the sleep from which he never awakened. This great doctor who had done so much for humanity by discovering insulin died as he had lived, in selfless service to others.

Jesus talked of such men: "Greater love hath no man than this, that a man lay down his life for his friends." Jesus Himself later did this, sacrificing His life for all the sins of this world. We admire men like Banting, but we adore Christ because He was not a mere man; He was God's only Son who came to die that we might live.

The premise of the gospel Christ preached is that we should selflessly serve Him. Jesus often talked of crosses to carry, burdens to bear, and enemies to love. He then said that if we obey His commands, we are indeed His friend and He ours. Love is not optional with the believer, however. "This is my commandment, That ye love one another, as I have loved you." The real believer is one who has given up his own selfishness to serve Christ and those about him. We are saved to serve.

45 Destiny

Before I formed thee in the belly I knew thee....
(Jer. 1:5)

Perhaps the most moving eulogy of Dr. Frederick Banting was one given at a gathering of the Diabetics Association: "Without Banting this meeting could have only been a gathering of ghosts bemoaning their fate." Dr. Banting was the main one responsible for the discovery of insulin which has extended the lives of millions of diabetics. Because Dr. Banting fulfilled his destiny, the world is a much better place in which to live.

God spoke explicitly to a young man centuries ago and told him his destiny. God said to Jeremiah: "Before I formed thee in the belly I knew thee; and before thou camest forth out of the womb I sanctified thee, and I ordained thee a prophet unto the nations." If Jeremiah had balked and refused to fulfill this destiny, we probably never would have known about Daniel and the three Hebrew children. All four were deeply influenced by Jeremiah's life.

God gives us the choice either to accept or reject our destiny. In Romans Paul said that God desires us to be conformed to the image of His Son. This is our destiny. If we move with it, our world will be a warmer and finer place to live. If we balk, many may fail to hear of our Lord and, like the diabetics, will be merely a gathering of ghosts bemoaning their fate.

46 Courtesy

Finally, be ye all of one mind, having compassion one of another, love as brethren, be pitiful, be courteous. (I Peter 3:8)

When actor Lloyd Bridges and his wife traveled East for a Broadway play, they left their fourteen-year-old son with friends. Mrs. Bridges says she was amazed and delighted to hear reports of how mannerly her son was being, but their first night home caused doubts. "He kept his head six inches from his plate, talked with his mouth full and ate his cake and ice cream with his knife. 'Son, I can't imagine what the Browns were talking about,' his father exclaimed. 'Your manners are horrible.' 'Gee, Dad!' sputtered our son, 'You don't think I eat this way when I'm with people!' "

Too often we tend to forget our manners at home. We must remember, however, that God's Word encourages us to be courteous even there. Any home where "Thank you" or "Please excuse me" are heard frequently is a pleasant home and fulfills at least one Bible admonition—Peter said we are to be just as concerned for the comfort of our family as for anyone.

Christian courtesy includes having compassion for one another, loving each other as brethren, being full of pity, and refusing to hurt back when we are hurt or yell back when we are yelled at. Peter's advice is very practical to homemakers. And as a married person himself he knew the pitfalls and problems.

47 Empathy

Rejoice with them that do rejoice, and weep with them that weep. (Rom. 12:15)

Not long ago a minister had to tell the parents of a twelve-year-old boy that he had drowned in a school outing. Later the parents told about that moment: "Rev. Allen didn't preach to us or tell us to be brave. He broke into tears and wept with us. We will always love him for that." This was the spirit Paul captured when he admonished believers to "rejoice with them that do rejoice, and weep with them that weep."

So many of us are afraid to show sentiment. Yet throughout God's Word are examples of great men who were moved to tears. David is the most vivid example, and even Christ wept over the city of Jerusalem. The Psalmist said, "They that sow in tears shall reap in joy. He that goeth forth and weepeth, bearing precious seed, shall doubtless come again with rejoicing, bringing his sheaves with him" (Ps. 126:5, 6).

We should resolve to show our sentiment today, as the opportunity arises. With those who have been most fortunate and are basking in the joy of recent accomplishments or blessings may we sincerely rejoice and thank God. With those whose hearts have been broken may we share their grief, feeling deeply for them and reaching out to them in love.

48 No News

But the natural man receiveth not the things of the Spirit of God: for they are foolishness unto him: neither can he know them, because they are spiritually discerned. (I Cor. 2:14)

"If newspapers would give less attention to crime, there would not be so much of it," the average person on the street says. In response to requests from civic groups and individuals who felt that vandals were doing it for the publicity, the news media in Iowa decided not to report any news of vandalism for ninety days. Then the police department released statistics showing 36.5 percent more vandalism than during the same three months of the year before.

Three things emerged from this experiment: first, turning one's back on a problem does not make it go away; second, an uninformed public often harbors a false sense of security; third, that which "sounds" logical is not always logical.

These three observations are also true in the spiritual realm. Turning our back on coming judgment does not erase that judgment. The Bible says, ". . . the soul that sinneth, it shall die." We also can be lured into a false sense of security through being ill informed about eternal values. And finally, "There is a way which seemeth right unto a man, but the end thereof are the ways of death" (Prov. 14:12). Natural man simply cannot perceive the things of God; only after we are born again do we have the proper perspective.

49 Foxhole

He that dwelleth in the secret place of the most High shall abide under the shadow of the Almighty. (Ps. 91:1)

During the last days of World War II, President Harry S. Truman was asked how he managed to bear up so calmly under the stress and strain of the Presidency. He answered that he had "a foxhole in my mind," and just as a soldier retreats into his foxhole for protection and respite, Truman periodically retreated into his own "mental foxhole" where he allowed nothing to bother him. He had taken the advice of Marcus Aurelius: "Constantly then give to thyself this retreat, and renew thyself."

While Truman's mental foxhole might have been a good retreat, there is an even better one "under the shadow of the Almighty." Psalm 91, one of the most beloved chapters of the Bible, tells of the place of security to which the believer can go. In this spiritual foxhole, nothing can harm or hurt him. The Psalmist said that God "is my refuge and my fortress . . . in him will I trust."

There are in our world some very real dangers. Not only are there physical dangers, there are spiritual ones. Even the most bold need the protection mentioned in this beautiful psalm, protection from "the terror by night, . . . the arrow that flieth by day, . . . the pestilence that walketh in darkness, [and] . . . the destruction that wasteth at noonday."

50 Reaching Out

Let brotherly love continue. (Heb. 13:1)

Often people ask Dr. Thomas P. Malone, a psychiatrist, what psychiatry is all about. His answer is, "Almost every emotional problem can be summed up in one particular bit of behavior—it's people walking around screaming 'for God's sake, love me.' He goes through a million different manipulations to get somebody to love him. On the other hand, healthy people are those who walk around looking for someone to love. And if you see changes in the people seeking for love, they give up their screaming for all their lives."

Dr. Malone's view of his role as a psychiatrist is certainly a noble and awesome one. He tries to get people to love one another. While psychiatry certainly has helped some to adjust, only Christ can so revolutionize character as to change a person from seeking to giving. Jesus came to this world to show men how to live. Through Christ we can learn how to give up our selfish seeking for attention and start giving ourselves to His kingdom.

Jesus told us that when we give up our lives, we find them. As we give up our selfish seeking and long to reach out in genuine love, we receive many blessings. No wonder it says in Hebrews, "Let brotherly love continue."

51 Partners

. . . be fruitful, and multiply, and replenish the earth, and subdue it. . . . (Gen. 1:28)

A small department in a large company was producing less than it should have. The management finally went to the employees and said, "Consider yourselves a partnership. Here is your budget for personnel. Hire whom you want and divide the money as you want. Just get the job done." The workers did just that and efficiency so increased that their salaries increased twenty-five percent. The point of the experiment was clear; a partnership works better than a pyramid in the business world.

In the very first chapter of the Bible we are told that we are in partnership with God. While God created the heavens and the earth, he left it to man to subject the earth. Note His instructions to Adam: ". . . be fruitful, and multiply, and replenish the earth, and subdue it. . . ." As the company did with their employees, God has done with us. He has given us ample talent and resources to subdue this earth and to be fruitful and multiply. We can only do this, however, through a right relationship with God.

Throughout Scripture we are reminded of our partnership with God. In prayer we are His partners. As we pray, His will is done on earth. We bind and we loose by our prayers. We are His representatives in witness. God did not send angels to tell the story of Christ; He sent us into all the world. We are workers together with God.

52 Building

For if these things be in you, and abound, they make you that ye shall neither be barren nor unfruitful in the knowledge of our Lord Jesus Christ. (II Peter 1:8)

The Ozark Mountain people have a saying: "A man don't know nothing he hasn't learned." In other words, we all start from the same level and build. Even genius depends on the data given it. William Shakespeare used playbooks to write his masterpieces. Mozart is said to have taken the opening theme of the overture *The Magic Flute* from a Clementi sonata. This does not diminish the genius of these men. It merely points out that their work stemmed from that of their predecessors.

In our work with the Lord, we must remember that every day is a building process in our lives. We are learning how to walk with Him. We were not born into the kingdom fully grown. In II Peter 1:8 Peter talked about that building process. He implied that we all start on the same level and "build" daily.

Our building materials are virtues such as faith, knowledge, and temperance. Others are patience, godliness, brotherly kindness, and charity. Peter said that as we give these virtues full sway in our lives we are fruitful, and as we ignore them we are barren. Peter's plea is clear: "Wherefore the rather, brethren, give diligence to make your calling and election sure: for if ye do these things, ye shall never fall" (II Peter 1:10).

53 Time

To every thing there is a season, and a time to every purpose under the heaven. (Eccles. 3:1)

Ardis Whitman tells of the death of a farmer's wife. She had been a good and busy mother, raising a family and toiling through the long days. At her funeral her husband did not weep, but he shuffled up to the pastor with a worn book in his hand. He said, "It's poems. She liked them. Would you read one for her now? She always wanted us to read them together, but I never had the time. Every day on the farm there were always things to do. But I got to thinking, nobody's doing them today and it doesn't seem to matter. I guess you don't get it into your head what time's for until it's too late."

Most of us abuse time rather than use it. The philosopher noted that when God made water He made it by the oceanfuls. He made flowers by the fieldfuls and stars by the heavenfuls. When He made time, however, He made it in day-tight compartments. We are wise if we learn to use time properly.

The Psalmist prayed, "So teach us to number our days, that we may apply our hearts unto wisdom" (90:12). We all feel guilty about our misuse of time. Let us ask God to give us a proper perspective on time. He can give us the wisdom to balance our time properly between our Lord, our family, our church, and our friends.

54 Soldier

Thou therefore endure hardness, as a good soldier of Jesus Christ. (II Tim. 2:3)

In 1919 President Woodrow Wilson proclaimed November 11 as Armistice Day to remind Americans of the tragedies of war. In 1971 Congress changed the date to the fourth Monday in October and the name to Veterans Day. Canada has set aside a similar day—Remembrance Day on November 11. Both countries seek to show appreciation for all who have given their service and their lives for the lands we love.

It is sad that there even have to be veterans. Veterans are made by wars, and wars mar the history of mankind. Yet war will be with us as long as man is in rebellion against God. Paul talks about another war being waged in the spirit world. The forces of Satan are pitted against the forces of our Lord and Christ. Paul admonished Timothy to be a good soldier for Christ and to endure hardness.

Christ never promised roses on the battlefield. We are involved in an intense spiritual warfare, and we will at times get weary. When it seems Satan has hit us with every weapon, we need to draw strength from Paul's words: "If we suffer, we shall also reign" with Christ (II Tim. 2:12).

55 Snakebite

*And he shook off the beast into the fire, and felt
no harm.* (Acts 28:5)

How the body digests food was first discovered on
Michigan's Mackinac Island. A worker for the American
Fur Company was accidentally shot in the stomach
while shopping at an island store in 1822. Fort Mackinac's Dr. William Beaumont managed to save the young
man's life, but the wound would not heal. As a result the
doctor was able to observe and later to experiment with
the previously unknown process of digestion. Those
experiments greatly advanced medical knowledge.

Even unpleasant things have their rewards. Paul,
shipwrecked on an island in the middle of the Mediterra-
nean, was gathering sticks for a fire. Suddenly a snake
bit him, and by all human understanding Paul should
have died. Yet God refused to let the snake harm the
apostle, and because of that event the islanders found
the Lord. God brought something beautiful out of Paul's
pain.

A poem says:
> *Two men looked between the bars;*
> *One saw the mud, the other the stars.*

This is especially meaningful for believers. No matter
what happens to us, we need only relax and let God
glorify Himself through it. We need not panic. God is
still on the throne. Let us look today at the stars and
leave the mud for those without faith.

56 No Fellowship

*And have no fellowship with the unfruitful works
of darkness, but rather reprove them.* (Eph. 5:11)

Superstition is still with us. On Mackinac Island is the
famous "Crack-in-the-Island" which according to Indian
legend descends to the depths of the "spirits of the
dead." The crack is said to be haunted by a giant demon
who tried to descend to the depths but was repulsed.
Now he clings desperately to the edge of the fissure, and
if you step on his fingers, calamities like sickness, loss of
wealth, and misfortune in love might befall you. The
legend is not taken seriously, but many today do believe
in superstition and the "black arts."

Today there is an alarming rise in witchcraft. And
there is a subtle campaign to improve the image of
witchcraft. Practitioners say that it is really a religion
and that they use only "white magic." Often they
attempt to blend elements of Christianity with their
incantations.

The problem is not new. It plagued the Ephesian
church. Ephesus was famous for the magical arts. Paul's
converts there burned about ten thousand dollars worth
of magic books. Later Paul wrote to encourage them to
keep separated from those involved in these magical arts.
In our day we too must draw the line very clearly. God's
Word tells us to have no fellowship with those involved
in these works of darkness. Superstitions flee in the face
of faith.

57 Free To Study

I must work the works of him that sent me, while it is day: the night cometh, when no man can work. (John 9:4)

At least three states have taken advantage of the Supreme Court's 1963 ruling that, while public schools cannot conduct sectarian worship services, they can provide objective instruction in religious beliefs, literature, and history. Michigan, Wisconsin, and California now have approved religious studies. Florida certifies teachers for objective instruction in Biblical literature. Similar courses are underway in several other states.

Just before his death Louis Cassels wrote: "This can happen in all states—if parents and church folk care enough. It is not the Constitution or the Supreme Court, but adult apathy which keeps America's youth in a state of religious illiteracy." Perhaps Mr. Cassels is right. We challenge everyone to encourage the inclusion of such courses in all of our schools.

At first we may meet opposition, but that should not stop us. Jesus felt an urgency about His ministry that defied discouragement. He knew the night was coming. May we feel the same urgency.

58 Wheels of Time

And I will strengthen them in the Lord; and they shall walk up and down in his name, saith the Lord. (Zech. 10:12)

A wise man observed: "The wheels of time have ratchets on them; they only move forward." Both the pleasures and pains of the past are gone, and we stand on the threshold of the future. Omar Khayyam lamented:

> *The moving finger writes; and having writ,*
> *moves on:*
> *Nor all your piety nor wit shall lure it back*
> *to cancel half a line,*
> *Nor all your tears wash out a word of it.*

Yet there is also something joyful about those ratchets on the wheels of time. Our past failures are behind us and are buried in the sea of God's forgetfulness. We have a new standard. This seems to be the message of Zechariah 10:12.

Israel's sins had cost them the promised land and brought much sorrow. Heartbroken, Zechariah pleaded with a wayward people to return to their God. He promised that if they did, God would give rain for their thirsty crops, tread down their enemies, strengthen their homes, return them to their land, and treat them as though they had never sinned. Zechariah climaxed the promise: "And I will strengthen them in the Lord; and they shall walk up and down in his name. . . ."

Many Christians are deeply pained by the past. Hurts of long ago still haunt them, and they never forget their failures. These heavy burdens keep them from their best and rob them of much joy. Remember the ratchets on the wheels of time. The past can be totally committed to Christ. We can live in the gladness of today.

59 Holding On

God is our refuge and strength, a very present help in trouble. (Ps. 46:1)

During my first airplane ride I held on. I looked out the window and the ground seemed so far away. I tensed every time the tiny plane hit an air pocket, desperately clenching the strap by the window. How ridiculous I must have looked to those more accustomed to air travel. After all, clinging to that strap will not help if the plane plummets to the earth.

While it amuses us to envision someone clinging tenaciously to a tiny strap in a moving plane, many are going through life just as frightened. They seem to wince at every turn and keep their hands on their pulse. Physicians estimate that 33,000 patients each week are not really sick, only afraid. Our generation is clinging to the strap and yet knows that it is not doing any good.

Some members of our generation have learned to live more relaxed. They too feel the bumps and see the perils. Yet they are confident that everything will be okay. They have learned that our security is in the Christ we love. "The Lord of hosts is with us; the God of Jacob is our refuge" (Ps. 46:7). Confident living comes not by human resolution but by a relationship to Christ. As we are in Christ we can be assured of His complete control of our lives. Then we can relax. Paul had learned to love Christ deeply: ". . . Christ shall be magnified in my body, whether it be by life, or by death" (Phil. 1:20). May each of us learn to live more confidently in Christ by fully trusting Him.

60 Unfinished Buildings

For if these things be in you, and abound, they make you that ye shall neither be barren nor unfruitful in the knowledge of our Lord Jesus Christ. (II Peter 1:8)

When trouble plagues them, the people of Rome say, "It's just like St. Peter's; it is never finished." They have resigned themselves to the fact that St. Peter's Basilica, a beautiful place of worship the construction of which was begun more than five hundred years ago, will never be completed. What may be true of St. Peter's is certainly true of a building about which the Bible talks.

Paul described the believer and his growth as "a field under God's cultivation, or, if you like, a house being built to his plan" (I Cor. 3:9 *Phillips*). Some seem to think the Christian springs fully grown from the womb of conversion. How wrong they are. God's Word repeatedly tells us that knowing Christ involves daily growth. It is as if each day God adds new building blocks to our lives. We help Him build by daily devoting ourselves and submitting to His will.

To build properly, nothing is ever left to chance. Therefore, Peter tells us exactly how God will help us grow. God adds to our faith virtue, then knowledge, then temperance, then patience, then godliness, then brotherly kindness, and finally love. Peter said something that staggers the mind: ". . . give diligence to make your calling and election sure: for if ye do these things, ye shall never fall" (II Peter 1:10). May we remember that God is working on and in our lives and building us for eternity.

61 Human Inventions

*. . . the Lord hath anointed me to preach good
tidings unto the meek . . . to bind up the brokenhearted, to proclaim liberty to the captives, and
the opening of the prison to them that are bound.*
(Isa. 61:1)

An angry black militant sneered, "If Christianity is a
valid religion, why is it so divided?" While his question is
not new, it deserves an answer. Christendom is divided
into Protestant and Roman Catholic, conservatives and
liberals. And even these groups are divided. Clearly there
is at best a cold war between some segments of the
kingdom. Why?

Perhaps the best answer is that God never intended
the great message of salvation to settle down into one
denomination, into narrowness or legalism. We must
understand that religious organizations are the inven-
tions of man rather than the creation of God.

While religious organizations are often necessary and
denominations provide valuable services, the believer
must remember that the message of Christ crosses over
man-made barriers to hear the hurt of humanity. Christ's
ministry was to preach the good tidings to the meek,
bind up the brokenhearted, proclaim liberty to the
captives, release from prison those who are bound, and
proclaim the coming of His kingdom. The wise believer
understands that religious organizations are often very
human and are only to speed the preaching of the great
gospel message. Too often we feud over unimportant
things. The believer patterns his ministry after that of
His Lord and seeks to bring people together rather than
separate them.

62 Our Oldest Man

I beseech you therefore, brethren, by the mercies of God, that ye present your bodies a living sacrifice, holy, acceptable unto God, which is your reasonable service. (Rom. 12:1)

Just a few months ago a man died who claimed to have been born eight years after George Washington died. Thomas Jefferson was president when Russian Shirali Muslimov came into the world, the fifteen-million-dollar Louisiana Purchase had been completed just two years before, Aaron Burr had gunned down Alexander Hamilton just one year before, and Johnny Appleseed was still planting trees across our land. Without question Muslimov died earth's oldest man in modern times.

Interestingly enough the only thing outstanding about Muslimov's life was its length. While he gained much fame for his longevity, others who have lived only a fraction as long have helped humanity much more. Clearly it is not so important how long one lives as how one lives. Man's life at its longest is still like fading flowers and passing shadows, and that is why Paul admonished believers to emphasize the really important thing. He asked us to present our bodies as living sacrifices to our God.

In our strife-torn and tension-filled age, God is still calling men to live right. There is an urgent need for men who love Christ and are sold out for the gospel. It really does not matter how long they live since they are building for eternity. Those who live well live forever.

63 Bad Religion

He hath shewed thee, O man, what is good; and
what doth the Lord require of thee, but to do
justly, and to love mercy, and to walk humbly
with thy God? (Mic. 6:8)

Religion is not necessarily a good thing, and religious
people are not inevitably good. Pascal wisely observed,
"Men never do evil so completely and cheerfully as when
they do it from a religious conviction." Examples are the
German extermination of the Jews and the holy wars
fought so savagely. Many of man's greatest atrocities
have been done in the name of religion, and this is what
prompted Micah to call Israel to repentance.

God's chosen people were hiding their evil behind a
cloak of religion. They tried to appease a just God with
elaborate offerings. But Micah asked, "Will the Lord be
pleased with thousands of rams, or with ten thousands
of rivers of oil? shall I give my firstborn for my
transgression, the fruit of my body for the sin of my
soul?" (Mic. 6:7). Religious activity means nothing to
God unless the heart is pure. Only after sin is forgiven
and justice is done do sacrifices please God.

Man has not really changed since the days of Micah.
He is still trying to buy God off with huge gifts of "good
works." Yet God still calls for man to be loving,
merciful, and just in his dealings. He asks for a right
relationship with the Creator and reminds us that not
everyone who calls Him "Lord" will be saved. Only
those whose lives are righteous and good are worthy to
be called His chosen ones.

64 The Coming King

Watch therefore: for ye know not what hour your Lord doth come. (Matt. 24:42)

Approximately one-fifth of the Bible is prophecy, and one-third of that concerns the second coming of Christ. Christ's second coming is mentioned eight times more than His first and twice as often as the atonement. One out of thirty verses in the New Testament concerns this great hope, and two New Testament books are almost entirely devoted to it. Without question the doctrine of the second coming is emphasized in God's Word and therefore is important to those who love the Lord.

Jesus spent much of His time telling about His second coming. He told many parables concerning this hope, including those of the "goodman" of the household, the faithful and wise servant, the ten virgins, and the talents. Throughout all these stories the predominant theme is the readiness of the believer for Christ's return. This readiness involves multiplying the talents He has entrusted to us. The faithful and good servants watch and work, redeeming the time until the Master returns.

In the classic book *The Robe* Justus keeps his ear tuned to the sky. He peers over each horizon and longingly looks for each daybreak. His constant thought is "Maybe the Master will return today." In this last day when our weary world totters on the brink of disaster, there is still the glorious fact that Christ will return for those awaiting His appearance. We have the word of our Lord that He is coming, and He has never broken a promise. As we look forward to this week and this year, may we like Justus say, "Could it be today?" We must work for our Lord as never before because the time is growing short.

65 The Glorious Hope

. . . and unto them that look for him shall he appear the second time without sin unto salvation. (Heb. 9:28)

Not long ago a famed scientist remarked, "The United States has 100,000 atomic weapons while Russia has 50,000. Yet, only four thousand such weapons destroy the entire human race." Another scientist said, "I am not optimistic that the human race will survive another ten years." Bertrand Russell bitterly added, "I wouldn't give a 50-50 chance that one person will be alive on this planet forty years from now." These winds of despair have blown across our dying planet until we all, living in an uneasy tension, wonder what shattering blow will hit us next. Pollution, scandal, and violence permeate our daily lives.

Man without God has absolutely no reason to hope. Without question our scientific accomplishments have outstripped our moral strength. We recklessly rattle rockets and threaten ourselves with total extinction. The picture is indeed bleak, and no relief is in sight. Pitted against the blackness of the hour, however, is the promise of centuries ago: "I will return." Christ promised to return to our world and bring order out of chaos, joy out of despair. This is the glorious hope of the believer. This is why we can rest well while others bite their fingernails.

Jesus taught His disciples to pray, "Thy kingdom come." What a remarkable petition this is. When Christ's kingdom comes, there will be no more war and hatred. Babies will not die of starvation and neglect. When Christ comes, human suffering will cease. No wonder the believer should daily pray, "Thy kingdom come." The believer longs for His Lord's return.

66 The "Snake Line"

He shall feed his flock like a shepherd: he shall gather the lambs with his arm, and carry them in his bosom, and shall gently lead those that are with young. (Isa. 40:11)

When a farmer buys land in New England, he often asks, "Is it above the snake line?" Experience has proven that there is a line above which snakes cannot live. Land above the "snake line" is protected by an unseen law of God from poisonous vipers. In the spiritual world there is also a "snake line." Below crawl all kinds of things that prey on the spiritual man and threaten to destroy him.

Job, wise to the ways of God, noted long ago, "There is a path which no fowl knoweth, and which the vulture's eye hath not seen: the lion's whelps have not trodden it, nor the fierce lion passed by it" (28:7, 8). This explains why many Christians rest peacefully while the world around them crumbles. They face death—their own and that of their families—with a calmness that cannot be explained. They are serene despite the winds of disaster blowing about them. All of us have known such persons, who without doubt have learned to live above the spiritual "snake line."

Below the "snake line" we are troubled by spiritual poverty, weariness, depletion, and other crawling vipers of Satan. Paul talked of sitting together in "heavenly places" above the cares of this world and the agony of spirit many experience. He told us we can be more than conquerors through Christ, who loved us. May we move today above the "snake line" and leave behind defeat and despair.

67 Rat on the Plane

If ye then be risen with Christ, seek those things which are above. . . . Set your affection on things above, not on things on the earth. (Col. 3:1, 2)

Flying over heavily wooded terrain, a pilot heard gnawing noises in the back of his small aircraft. Panic gripped him as he realized that a rat was chewing through wires vital to the plane's operation. By the time he could get to an airport it might be too late. Then an idea struck him. He nosed his airplane as high as he could without losing consciousness and put on his oxygen mask. In just a few minutes the gnawing stopped and the rat was dead.

Many shuffle through life with gnawing doubt, fears, guilts, and inferiorities until these things overcome them. They have tried many ways to get rid of these overwhelming naggings, but all have failed. One thing, however, has never failed. When we nose the craft of our lives upward, real relief is ours. Isaiah promised that those who "wait upon the Lord shall renew their strength; they shall mount up with wings as eagles; they shall run, and not be weary; and they shall walk, and not faint" (Isa. 40:31). Doubts, fears, guilts, and inferiorities cannot last in the pure presence of our Christ.

The Psalmist added, "Thou wilt shew me the path of life: in thy presence is fulness of joy; at thy right hand there are pleasures for evermore" (16:11). When doubts return to gnaw at us, it is time to nose heavenward to bask again in His presence. These "rats" of doubt die as we soar higher and higher into the pure presence of Christ.

68 Little Things

His Lord said unto him, Well done, thou good and faithful servant: thou hast been faithful over a few things, I will make thee ruler over many things. . . . (Matt. 25:21)

Many years ago a wise poet observed:
> *I thought, if defeat came at all,*
> *It would be as a big bold definite joust,*
> *With a cause or a name.*
> *And it came.*
> *I had not thought the daily skirmish*
> *With a few details worthwhile;*
> *And so I turned my back upon them*
> *Year on year; until one day*
> *A million minutes blanketed together,*
> *Rose up and overwhelmed me.*

Jesus told a parable about little things that are important to our lives. Talents had been given to men, and now judgment day was upon them. Those who had been faithful in everyday business brought earned talents to the master. The one who had ignored daily responsibilities brought nothing. To each of the faithful ones Jesus said, ". . . thou hast been faithful over a few things, I will make thee ruler over many. . . ."

Only after we have been faithful with what we have where we are does God move us into a greater ministry. Joseph had to prove himself first in slavery and then in prison before God trusted him with the fate of two major nations. What we do with what we have is vital to our future. Thus the faithful followers of Christ take care of the little things and sow loving acts of kindness and goodness in their homes and neighborhoods and on their jobs. They are careful to give the cup of water and to love. These wise ones will have much to give the Master when He returns.

69 Victorious Living

Being then made free from sin, ye became the servants of righteousness. (Rom. 6:18)

Dr. Freda S. Kehm tells of the seven-year-old who complained, "How come I always get blamed for everything I do." The child psychologist adds that at this age a child is very conscious of "being blamed." Feelings of guilt are not confined to seven-year-olds. All of us struggle with them and even Paul the apostle complained, "For the good that I would I do not: but the evil which I would not, that I do" (Rom. 7:19). This poignant verse captures the plight of mortal man, his eternal struggle against evil.

If Paul experienced these two natures pulling against each other, so does every other Christian. Indeed evil is ever with us and usually we are blamed for everything that we do. Does this mean that we cannot live above sin? No! Paul added that Jesus Christ is the answer to the problem, and when He lives in our hearts, He takes over and lives through us. Paul could then say, "There is therefore now no condemnation to them which are in Christ Jesus, who walk not after the flesh, but after the Spirit" (Rom. 8:1).

We are often tempted to do evil. Within ourselves we cannot possibly resist. Yet when Christ takes over, He breaks the bonds of lust, passion, and pride and makes us servants of righteousness. No longer do we need despair, burdened by the weight of sin. We can indeed become "free" and live as God intended, no longer pulled down by fleshly passions. The struggle ends at Calvary.

70 Demon of Fear

There is no fear in love; but perfect love casteth out fear: because fear hath torment. He that feareth is not made perfect in love. (I John 4:18)

The United States has more cases of extreme mental disorders per capita than any other nation. Statistics reveal that one of every twenty Americans can expect to be institutionalized for mental illness, and one family in five will be touched by mental disorder. Those who spend their lives trying to determine the reason for these frightening statistics say that the most frequent cause of mental illness is fear. Frankly, Americans are terrified.

All fear is not bad. One kind of fear motivates us, keeping us from jumping off buildings and burning ourselves to death. This fear, which keeps us physically and spiritually healthy, is the fear which moved Noah to build the ark. It is the "fear of the Lord." However, another kind of fear dominates us, and it is destructive. It literally drives men crazy, tormenting them and making them live in constant dread. This fear takes a heavy toll in heart victims, suicides, and alcoholics, and it must be conquered if man is to know peace.

As always, the answer to this problem is in God's Word. John said the antidote for fear is perfect love. As we learn to love Christ more and actualize that love in our relationships with people, fear is crowded from our lives: ". . . perfect love casteth out fear. . . ." Even some believers have not yet learned to live without fear. John patiently told them, "He that feareth is not made perfect in love." But as we continue to expose ourselves to the Lord, love begins to force out nagging and destructive fears.

71 The First Revival

And he said unto him, If thy presence go not with me, carry us not up hence. (Exod. 33:15)

The world's first revival was at Sinai. While Moses was in the presence of God receiving the commandments, the people he led were dancing naked before a pagan idol. In anger Moses rebuked them and called for repentance. He reminded them that while they had come out of Egypt, Egypt had not come out of them. Sorrow gripped their hearts, an extended prayer meeting took place, and a revival swept through Israel.

Three important factors contributed to this national revival. First, there was repentance. Moses had told God that unless He went with them to the promised land, they would not go. In earnest prayer he repented for the people and then called them to repent. They became convicted, and in humble prayer they pleaded for forgiveness. Next, a "tent of meeting" was pitched outside the camp. People came daily to pray, and their hunger for God burned in their midst. In the heat of that spiritual atmosphere, God revived each person. The final factor was intercessory prayer. Moses prayed when he learned of the Israelites' sin, confessing their sins daily, pleading with God to forgive them. As a result of the Sinai revival, the people destroyed their idols from Egypt; they repudiated any return to slavery; and they became God's voice for their day.

The revival that swept Sinai can sweep our lands in this last day before Jesus returns. North America can tear down her idols, break loose from her slavery to sin, and become God's voice in these last days. God's people can bring this about through prayer.

72 Like Sheep

All we like sheep have gone astray; we have turned every one to his own way; and the Lord hath laid on him the iniquity of us all. (Isa. 53:6)

Homing pigeons can be released as many as one thousand miles from home, and they still will find their way back. For this reason they were used during wars as messengers. Bees have the same sense of direction, and when taken miles away from their beehive, "make a bee-line" back. Some animals have a sense of direction that cannot be confused, but one animal without any sense of direction whatever is the sheep.

Sheep can get lost within yards of their destination. They wander, and unless they are found they usually end up dead or in deep trouble. Men are much like sheep. Isaiah wrote, "All we like sheep have gone astray. . . ." Man does not have any innate sense of moral guidance, as the modern-day fear of nuclear war, riots, and murder testifies. Man cannot set his own morals just as he cannot set his own watch.

God's Word adds for the arrogant, "If we say that we have no sin, we deceive ourselves, and the truth is not in us" (I John 1:8). Again, "For all have sinned, and come short of the glory of God. . . ." (Rom. 3:23). The ways in which we sin might differ, but we all stray: ". . . we have turned every one to his own way. . . ." What tempts some will not tempt others, yet each of us has a character flaw that separates us from God.

Far more important than admitting we are sinners, however, is the fact that we can be "found." The Lord has laid on Christ the sins of us all. The Good Shepherd comes into our lives, gives us a sense of direction, and rescues us from the destruction of sin. As long as He leads us, we need fear no evil.

73 No Place To Hide

My substance was not hid from thee, when I was made in secret, and curiously wrought in the lowest parts of the earth. (Ps. 139:15)

There are three things from which no one can escape: one's shadow, oneself, and God. Every child probably has tried to run from his shadow and has found it impossible. A famed philosopher, explaining why a certain rich man was constantly unhappy even while traveling around the world, said, "Everywhere he goes he takes himself with him." And God's Word lets us know we cannot escape God: "Whither shall I go from thy spirit? or whither shall I flee from thy presence?"

While to some the constant presence of God is frightful, to the believer it is a great comfort. The sinner finds no bottle deep enough, no drug trip long enough, no excess sufficient to keep God away or to quiet his nagging conscience. He is ever haunted because God created in him a God-shaped void that can be filled with nothing or no one else. The believer, on the other hand, finds no pleasure, joy, or happiness apart from His Lord.

David, deep in thought, confessed, "If I ascend up into heaven, thou art there: if I make my bed in hell, behold, thou art there. If I take the wings of the morning, and dwell in the uttermost parts of the sea; even there shall thy hand lead me, and thy right hand shall hold me" (Ps. 139:8-10). The great poet added that although God saw his imperfections, yet "how precious also are thy thoughts unto me, O God! how great is the sum of them!" (Ps. 139:17). No wonder David could relax, enjoying the sheer joy of God's nearness. Only those who have something to hide, hide from God. The true believer loves and longs for the presence of the ever-present One.

74 The Cover Off

Blessed is he that readeth, and they that hear the words of this prophecy, and keep those things which are written therein: for the time is at hand. (Rev. 1:3)

Astrology is now a fifty-million-dollar American business. People seem unsatisfied with science and disillusioned with technology, and are looking for something or someone to reveal the future to them. A revival of witchcraft is sweeping our land and Satan cults are springing up everywhere. For such an hour God's Word declares, "And when they shall say unto you, Seek unto them that have familiar spirits, and unto wizards that peep, and that mutter: should not a people seek unto their God? . . ." (Isa. 8:19).

Perhaps the book of the Bible that most helps us understand our day and its confusion is Revelation. Many have felt they cannot understand this difficult book and therefore read it little. Its very title, however, comes from a Greek word which means "to take off the cover." It is a "revelation," not an enigma. And this is the only book of the Bible which promises that those who read it in particular will be blessed. In this fascinating book we can see our age mirrored and the events of the end which are swiftly taking place. In fact the phrase "which must shortly come to pass" (Rev. 1:1) means in the original Greek that when these events start, they will be fulfilled rapidly. We cannot afford to neglect this important book if we really want to hear what the Spirit is saying to the church.

During the next twelve months, if Jesus tarries, it would be wise to read Revelation through several times. Doing this will tune our hearts to the Spirit and show us that our redemption is near.

75 Finished

... that I may know him, and the power of his resurrection, and the fellowship of his sufferings, being made conformable unto his death. (Phil. 3:10)

Someone once asked Rembrandt how he knew when a painting is finished. The great master replied, "A picture is finished when it expresses the artist's intention." Christians are much the same; we stop growing only when we fully express the Master's intentions. No one can say that his life is perfect in every respect. Therefore, all of us still have a lot of growing to do. Paul the apostle admitted: "Not as though I had already attained, either were already perfect: but I follow after, if that I may apprehend that for which also I am apprehended of Christ Jesus" (Phil. 3:12).

Tragically some have given up, saying their lives never will express the meaning of the Master. Like Michelangelo's unfinished statue of Matthew, they feel the stone of their lives will not yield to the chisel of the Sculptor. How sad these are. While the clay is imperfect, the hands of the Potter are skilled. He can and will take the material of our lives and complete us as He desires.

May we realize that those things which come into our lives the Master is using to shape us. He is finishing us according to His plan, and one day, if we are faithful, our lives will indeed express everything He wants them to. Paul encourages us to forget past failures and reach ahead "unto those things which are before" (Phil. 3:13). Christ's work in us proceeds every day.

76 Starving Americans

Ho, every one that thirsteth, come ye to the waters, and he that hath no money; come ye, buy, and eat; yea, come, buy wine and milk without money and without price. (Isa. 55:1)

Millions of Americans with money in the bank are starving. While Americans spend more than 110 billion dollars for food annually, experts say much of the food is merely "empty calories." Dr. Jean Mayer observes, "Your body needs a certain amount of vitamins A, C, D, and iron per pound of body weight regardless of how much food you take in." Most of the food advertised is "exotic food" with little nutritional value.

What is true in the physical is also true in the spiritual. Isaiah long ago asked, "Wherefore do ye spend money for that which is not bread? and your labour for that which satisfieth not? hearken diligently unto me, and eat ye that which is good, and let your soul delight itself in fatness" (Isa. 55:2). In our modern age we feed our spirits and minds much "food," but very little of it is spiritually nutritional.

Television, radio, newspapers, and books offer us all sorts of mental food, but most of it is "empty calories" and will starve us to death. Amos foretold: "Behold, the days come, saith the Lord God, that I will send a famine in the land, not a famine of bread, nor a thirst for water, but of hearing the words of the Lord. . . ." (8:11). We have lived to see that spiritual starvation. May believers everywhere vow to feed on that which is spiritually and morally uplifting.

77 The One Who Brings

He first findeth his own brother Simon, and saith
unto him, We have found the Messias, which is,
being interpreted, the Christ. (John 1:41)

Men often are measured by their ability to move the
masses, and the Churchills, the Lincolns, the Roosevelts,
the Ghandis, the Hitlers, and the Stalins can do this.
Others, however, change the course of history through
gentle influence. Andrew was such a man.

Everybody remembers Andrew's brother. Some consider Andrew's only significance to be the fact that he
was related to Peter. God's Word, however, gives this
quiet disciple a special place, noting that he always
was bringing someone to Jesus. First he brought his
brother. Peter probably never would have sought the
Lord by himself, but Andrew brought him and Peter was
saved; Peter became one of the greatest forces in the
early church. Next, the Bible records that Andrew
brought to Jesus the boy with the little lunch. While the
other disciples were fretting because there was no food,
Andrew found the lad with the loaves and brought him
to his Lord. Finally, Andrew brought the Greeks to
Jesus just before the crucifixion. In that last week of our
Lord's life Andrew was still seeking people for the
Savior. What a dynamic believer, one who brings people
to Christ.

Maybe not much will be remembered about us in the
annals of history. Our names may never rank with those
who move the masses. But our lives will be significant if
we move the ones, the twos, the threes to come to the
Savior we love. As Andrew had a special place in the
heart of our Lord, we can too by bringing men and
women to Him. Note that Andrew began with his
family. That is always a good place to start.

78 The Eternal Debt

I am debtor both to the Greeks, and to the Barbarians; both to the wise, and to the unwise. (Rom. 1:14)

After long years of working and saving, some men brag, "I don't owe anything to anybody." The real believer can never say that. Paul forever settled our responsibility by saying, "I am [a] debtor. . . ." Later he observed, "Owe no man any thing, but to love one another: for he that loveth another hath fulfilled the law" (Rom. 13:8). The Christian is never really free from debt; he always owes his love.

Bound to his "love debt," Paul proceeded to give his life for those about him. He traveled the world preaching the gospel to both Jews and Gentiles. He discharged his responsibility to Greeks and barbarians. And because he paid his debt, we are still reaping the benefits. We are probably Christians today because Paul was responsible enough to travel to Europe and preach the gospel of our Lord. Thank God he never felt free from his obligation.

In these last days many of God's people are feeling the same responsibility Paul did. They realize how very much they owe the world the privilege of hearing the gospel and finding Christ as Lord. Because they are faithfully fulfilling their debt, millions have come into the kingdom. Only as people like Paul recognize their responsibility can the world be won to the Lord. We owe a debt, both to those at home and those across the sea. We owe a debt to the cultured "up-and-outers" as well as the crass "down-and-outers." May we pay our debt.

79 Freedom's Responsibility

Stand fast therefore in the liberty wherewith Christ hath made us free, and be not entangled again with the yoke of bondage. (Gal. 5:1)

Freedom is fragile. When the Congo declared its freedom a few short years ago, riots ensued in which more than a half million people were murdered. Some were so unaware of what freedom was that they brought boxes to political rallies to carry home their new "freedom." Freedom can be lost very easily. Jesus told of the prodigal son who fell into bondage because he did not know how to handle a lack of accountability.

Some freedoms spell failure: freedom from study, planning, work, discipline, and responsibility. Paul was careful to warn the young church to guard its new-found freedom in Christ. He saw that after being freed from the numberless laws of the Old Testament, one could use that freedom wrongly: "For, brethren, ye have been called unto liberty; only use not liberty for an occasion to the flesh, but by love serve one another" (Gal. 5:13).

In case any believer is confused about his new-found freedom, Paul outlined in Galatians 5 the fruit of the flesh and the fruit of the Spirit. If indeed the believer's life produces the fruit of the Spirit, he need not worry about abusing freedom. Paul adds, "If we live in the Spirit, let us also walk in the Spirit" (Gal. 5:25).

80 Saints and Swine

Let not then your good be evil spoken of. (Rom. 14:16)

After three harrowing years in a Nazi prison camp, Viktor Frankl said, "I saw some men act like swine while others acted like saints." The prominent psychiatrist explained that those who acted like saints had decided to act and react responsibly regardless of the conditions. Our everyday conduct depends on the same kind of decision.

Some have little concern for the feelings of others. Even some Christians feel it is no one's business what they do, and they live very selfishly. How foreign to the laws of love our Master taught. Paul pleaded, "But if thy brother be grieved with thy meat, now walkest thou not charitably. Destroy not him with thy meat, for whom Christ died" (Rom. 14:15). In other words, our actions should be geared to heal people, not hurt them. We are not islands, complete in ourselves, but oceans washing many shores.

Admittedly it is often difficult to decide what is right and wrong. These three criteria help us decide: (1) Can I do it with pure motives? (2) Will it offend anyone? (3) Will it expose me to the danger of developing bad habits? An honest answer to each question will make a sound decision easier.

The world is waiting for a people who live not by the law of the jungle but by the law of love. To a spiritually starving world, that is without doubt our best personal witness.

81 Horatio Alger

. . . and he turned again into the camp: but his servant Joshua, the son of Nun, a young man, departed not out of the tabernacle. (Exod. 33:11)

Everyone likes a success story. Horatio Alger stories told of the rise of a home-town boy to the pinnacles of success. All of us can identify with those who go from obscurity to fame without sacrificing their principles. Let us look at the secret of success of one of the most powerful and prominent men who ever lived.

Born in the small tribe of Ephraim, Joshua eventually became an aide of Moses and then Israel's leader during the conquest of the promised land. He was perhaps the greatest military man who ever lived. Scripture hints in Exodus 33:11 why Joshua became such a powerful leader. When all the others left for home from a prayer meeting, Joshua stayed and sought the Lord. No doubt in these moments God spoke to the young man's heart and gave him the burning hunger for the things of God that never left him. It was natural for the mantle of leadership to fall on him because he was ready spiritually.

In our uncertain century there is still room for youths who hesitate leaving God's house of prayer. And every person, young or old, can have that dynamic ministry of waiting before God for the souls of men. The greatest revival this world has ever known can and will come through prayer. We, like Joshua, must not depart from the tabernacle.

82 Haven for Ships

Zebulun shall dwell at the haven of the sea; and he shall be for an haven of ships; and his border shall be unto Zidon. (Gen. 49:13)

Henry Drummond, a famous Scottish preacher, commented, "The trouble with the religious is that they often care more for religion than humanity. Christ cared more for humanity than religion. Rather, His care for humanity was the chief expression of His religion." Drummond's charge is often true when we let our organizations or creeds overshadow our compassion. God's Word indicates that Zebulun never let this happen.

When Jacob blessed his children just before he died, he said many sad things about some. Simeon and Levi had been instruments of cruelty, and Reuben had disappointed him terribly. Of Zebulun, however, he fondly said, "Zebulun . . . shall be for an haven for ships. . . ." In other words, the great heart and compassion of Zebulun offered rest to the traveler weary of being tossed about and threatened by the heavy seas. His personality appealed to those who seek the security of a harbor. What an epithet to place over any man's life: "A haven for ships."

What makes some men attract and others repel those seeking help? Kindness is the key. One of the Proverbs notes, "The desire of a man is his kindness. . . ." (19:22). In other words, that which makes a man desirable is his kindness to those about him. Kindness makes a person approachable. The hurt one, seeking help, opens his heart to one who is kind. He knows he will not be condemned or rejected. The world needs more harbors and fewer coral reefs on which so many ships have dashed. Each of us should pledge to be more accessible, more loving, more tender, and more kind.

83 Kittens in a Basket

But seek ye first the kingdom of God, and his righteousness; and all these things shall be added unto you. (Matt. 6:33)

Coping with all the problems of our modern age is like putting kittens in a basket: just as you get one in, one pops out. It seems that when we get one problem solved, another confronts us. Sometimes we question if it all is worthwhile and are tempted to despair. God's Word speaks clearly to us at these times.

Jesus tasted of humanity and experienced the daily problems that overwhelm us. In the Sermon on the Mount He discussed them and gave us keys to solving them. First, He said not to worry, because the heavenly Father knows our bodily needs. Then He noted that we are not to fret continually because this does not help. He reminded us that God clothes the flowers of the field and cares for the birds of the air. He concluded that "if God so clothe the grass of the field, which to day is, and to morrow is cast into the oven, shall he not much more clothe you, O ye of little faith?" (Matt. 6:30).

We spend much of our time fretting and stewing about things the Master is fully aware of and has promised already to handle. If we seek His kingdom first, He will provide. He does this in many ways, and one is to give us clear and confident minds so we can discover new ways to meet our own needs. The mind free from nagging doubts and fears is creative. Paul acquired this confidence so that even when things went wrong he could say, "And we know that all things work together for good to them that love God, to them who are the called according to his purpose" (Rom. 8:28).

84 Men Who Almost Were

And when Jesus saw that he answered discreetly, he said unto him, Thou art not far from the kingdom of God. And no man after that durst ask him any question. (Mark 12:34)

History is filled with men who almost made it. Not long ago a teacher asked, "What do Charles Pinckney, Horatio Seymour, Alton Parker, and James Cox have in common?" No one knew. Each man ran for the United States presidency, Pinckney against Jefferson, Seymour against Grant, Parker against Teddy Roosevelt, and Cox against Harding. But history does not reward the man who almost succeeds, only the one who does succeed. God's Word also tells about men who almost made it but failed. An unnamed scribe is a case in point.

This brilliant young man approached Jesus and asked Him what was the greatest commandment. Jesus' answer was the most profound condensation of God's law: man is to love God with all his heart and his fellow man as himself. Apparently the scribe was deeply moved. He responded, "Well, Master, thou hast said the truth. . . ." (Mark 12:32). The Bible says that "when Jesus saw that he answered discreetly, he said unto him, Thou art not far from the kingdom of God. . . ." (Mark 12:34). The tragedy is that although he was not far, he evidently did not make it in.

The rich young ruler is another example, as is King Agrippa, who admitted he was "almost persuaded." These men apparently died near the door but not inside it. Our world is full of religious men who are so close yet so far. They too stand in danger of never really making it in. We should pray that they will move closer to committing themselves to the Master, and that we also will be totally committed to Him.

85 Failures

Only Luke is with me. Take Mark, and bring him with thee: for he is profitable to me for the ministry. (II Tim. 4:11)

A young businessman recently took his life because he could not face failure. His prosperous business started to fail, and when every effort to rescue it fell short, he shot himself, leaving a family to weep. It is true that our society exacts a heavy toll from people who fail. While we do not tolerate them and look with disdain on them, how wonderful that God does not adopt the same attitude. He is in the business of restoring failures.

A classic example of total failure was young John Mark. Pampered by his benevolent uncle, he traveled with him and Paul on a missionary journey. But he became homesick and cried until he got to go home. This apparently infuriated Paul. When John Mark later wanted to rejoin the team, Paul would not let him and even traded sharp words with Uncle Barnabas. Paul and Barnabas even separated over the matter. Mark was marked as a failure, and nobody wanted him as their minister. God, however, restored this young man to a place of great influence. How thrilling it must have been to receive the message from Paul, "Bring Mark, for he is useful to me." Out of failure God had raised a young giant. John Mark continued to be used, and today he is well known by the Gospel which bears his name.

Looking back over our lives we are often tempted to count the failures and feel so worthless. May we remember, however, that God restores failures and makes great witnesses of them. From our deepest heart we rejoice because we who have failed and come short of His glory have been restored to fellowship by Christ.

86 Never Give Up

We are troubled on every side, yet not distressed;
we are perplexed, but not in despair. (II Cor. 4:8)

A one-time doctor in Missouri is now a shipping clerk in a midwestern book store. Apparently things became so difficult for him in the medical profession that he gave up and settled for something far below his capabilities. In the crucible of crisis, many men quit rather than face the difficulties. They are overwhelmed by circumstances and live the rest of their lives defeated. Paul the apostle was never like this.

Pitted against the ugliness of the world, Paul preached the gospel at all costs. Five times he received thirty-nine lashes. He was struck with rods three times and stoned once. For 1½ days he clung to a tiny board in the churning sea after being shipwrecked. He spent many sleepless nights preaching and praying, and was rejected by some of those he counted friends. Yet Paul said eloquently, "For our light affliction, which is but for a moment, worketh for us a far more exceeding and eternal weight of glory...." (II Cor. 4:17). Paul would never give up.

While we probably have never had to face what the famed apostle did, there are still times we feel like quitting. At these times may we remember Paul's tenacity and endure hardness as a good soldier. Paul reminded us in another book that we will reap if we do not faint. Only he who finishes, however, receives the reward. In our moments of discouragement, may we never lose heart. Christ indeed is in us, and these afflictions are only momentary. God is with us not merely in good times, but at all times! Lift up your heart; we have a King!

87 The Still

Be still, and know that I am God: I will be exalted among the heathen, I will be exalted in the earth.
(Ps. 46:10)

On many British vessels when disaster strikes, "the still" is sounded. This signals people to pause a moment and figure out the wise thing to do. Panic, sailors feel, can be avoided if "the still" is observed. God gives us similar advice. Rather than panicking when crisis comes, we are to "be still, and know that I am God...." Perhaps that could be paraphrased, "Just don't be frightened; see how I can help you in this trying situation." The wise believer will learn to observe "the still" in times of tension.

If we are still only in times of trial, we miss much of what God is trying to say to us. We feel we do not have time to be still, but a recent University of Wisconsin study revealed that the average person spends three years of life waiting. How we use that time will determine much of our future. The wise person will use it to get to know God better, and he also will seek to get alone and listen to the quiet voice of the Creator.

Poems are not written on busy street corners, and symphonies are not composed in crowds. Aloneness is necessary for creativity and spiritual creation. So often we are spiritual chatterboxes when we come to the closet of prayer. How well it would be to learn to listen in those quiet moments "and know that I am God." Psalm 46 also states that "the heathen raged." How often we rage at this and that, and how much better if we listen to God. Let us relax and know Him, be still and learn to love Him better.

88 Warming Rays

But the wisdom that is from above is first pure,
then peaceable, gentle, and easy to be intreated,
full of mercy and good fruits, without partiality,
and without hypocrisy. (James 3:17)

The biting wind of winter makes us draw our wraps around us tightly, and when the warm and gentle rays of the sun envelop us in the spring, we take off our coats and bask in them. Similarly, a person who is cold and blustery repels us, and one who is open and warm makes it easy for us to open up and trust him with the secrets of our lives. For this reason Paul admonished believers to be open and warm.

Paul was not perfect. No doubt he was haunted by the bitter battle with Barnabas which broke up their effective missionary team. He was probably drawing on this experience when he encouraged believers to be gentle and tender with one another. He did not want them to suffer the same pangs of remorse that bothered him because he had acted so contrary to the Lord's desires.

God is gentle. David said, ". . . thy gentleness hath made me great" (II Sam. 22:36). One of Christ's most outstanding characteristics on earth was His gentleness. We who desire to be Christlike need to be the same. Two things often keep us from gentleness: sickness or pain, which make us sharp with others; and sin against us, which makes us vengeful. We need to carefully guard our spirits and ask God to make us gentle people.

89 Divided Heart

Teach me thy way, O Lord; I will walk in thy truth: unite my heart to fear thy name. (Ps. 86:11)

The story of the mule caught in indecision between two piles of hay is a classic. The poor animal moved toward one pile to eat, only to be distracted by the aroma from the other. Back and forth he went until he starved to death. One might doubt the historicity of the story, but not the truth it illustrates. One who remains between two strong forces weakens his position and dissipates his effectiveness. Jesus said we cannot serve God and mammon.

On Mt. Carmel Elijah asked Israel, "How long halt ye between two opinions? if the Lord be God, follow him: but if Baal, then follow him" (I Kings 18:21). Joshua demanded, ". . . choose you this day whom ye will serve." The Psalmist prayed, ". . . unite my heart to fear thy name." A divided heart spells disaster and defeat; the single-minded heart dedicated to Christ brings victory and power.

Many things demand our attention, and we often get wrapped up in interesting but rather unimportant things. Sometimes the business of living saps so much of our strength that we have only leftovers for the Lord. Some even try to give the Lord some time and money but not all of their hearts. The wise person realizes he cannot serve two masters, and he dedicates his whole life to the Lord. This means even his "secular" decisions are made only after asking the Lord's advice. The united heart never forgets to press "toward the mark." Pledge today that even in small decisions we first will seek the Lord's will.

90 Symbols

But these are written, that ye might believe that Jesus is the Christ, the Son of God; and that believing ye might have life through his name. (John 20:31)

Americans are intrigued by symbols. The city of Phoenix, for example, gets its name from the ancient symbol of resurrection. The mythical Phoenix bird died and exploded in fire. Out of the ashes arose a new bird. City fathers felt this legend expressed the city's rise from the burning desert. The olive branch has always symbolized peace; a palm, victory; an anchor, faith and hope; a peacock, immortality. In the early church the fish symbolized Christian faith because the five letters of the Greek word *fish* formed an acrostic meaning "Jesus Christ, Son of God, Savior."

In the New Testament four things symbolize eternal truths: the manger, the cross, the empty tomb, and the trumpet. They burn the truths deeply into our minds. The manger symbolizes God's eternal love for man in giving His only begotten Son; the cross, man's release from sin through the blood of Christ shed in His sacrificial death; the empty tomb, God's eternal existence; and the trumpet, Jesus' return for those who await His appearing. Our hearts are stirred when we think of these symbols of our Savior.

The manger is present in all contemporary nativity scenes, and crosses are worn as necklaces, charm bracelets, and key chains. Unfortunately, the empty tomb and the trumpet are not as prominent. These symbols are most meaningful to believers, however. Someday Jesus will come back so we can live with Him forever. All the world is waiting for that redemption.

91 Past Feeling

. . . being past feeling [they] have given themselves over unto lasciviousness, to work all uncleanness with greediness. (Eph. 4:19)

In 1906 a beautiful baby boy was born into a German home. As a child he was sensitive to the things of the Lord, but as a young adult he became very bitter. At twenty-six he joined the Nazi party, and he became known as the butcher of Germany. Adolf Eichmann murdered six million Jews and bragged, "I will leap into my grave laughing." When he was captured and tried a few years ago, he had not changed. He was executed, and he died as he lived, a bitter and evil man, sneering, "Regrets are for small children." Here is a vivid example of a man "past feeling."

God's Word warns that this can happen, and when it does, hell spills over on our world. The Hitlers and Stalins were once children with tender feelings, but something happened along the way to drain them of all consciousness of God and compassion for man. Little by little they stopped caring until they were "beyond feeling."

Because it is urgent that men sustain compassion and love for God, preachers plow the fallow ground of people's hearts. This is why ministers urge people to give and be compassionate. The only antidote to men like Eichmann is men of love. We should examine ourselves to see if we are still moved by the hurt of humanity. Dr. Pierce often says, "Break my heart with the things that break the heart of God." This prayer reminds us that believers are to be caring people. Those who have shut off the flow of compassion will die in bitterness; those who love God and men will live forever. The Bible says, "They that sow in tears shall reap in joy" (Ps. 126:5).

92 Explosion

*This is the stone which was set at nought of you
builders, which is become the head of the corner.*
(Acts 4:11)

The crowd around the cross would meet again. Pilate,
Herod, Annas, and Caiaphas thought it was all over when
they buried Jesus, but how wrong they were! The priests
had taken all precautions. Soldiers guarding the tomb
were paid off. Followers of Jesus were disbanded and
worshipers threatened. Christ, who had risen from the
dead, was missing; some said He had ascended.

Fifty days after the crucifixion and ten days after the
alleged ascension, the city of Jerusalem was astounded
by the most dramatic event in its history. Thousands
thronged near a tiny upper-story room where 120 believers had been secretly praying and waiting. From that
meeting was to come a missionary effort that would
reach the entire world. A spiritual explosion occurred
that the priests and officials could never contain. God's
Holy Spirit had filled these believers, and they would
charge through the world with the glorious news.

Because they were filled with the Holy Spirit, they
spoke boldly about Christ; people recognized they had
been with Jesus; and they could not keep silent even
though threatened, beaten, and jailed. Even during
persecution they prayed for power rather than deliv-
erance. The entire world would be shaken by these
believers. Today, before Christ returns, we can move our
world as those men did theirs. Jesus—the same yester-
day, today, and forever—can fill us so full of the Holy
Spirit that we too can speak boldly, show by our
countenance we have been with Christ, and be so
overjoyed with the Lord that we cannot help but tell
what we have seen and heard.